THE ULTIMATE FOODI 2-BASKET AIR FRYER COOKBOOK FOR BEGINNERS

1500 Days of Delicious and Easy Recipes for Home cooking using DualZone

Technology|Full Color Pictures Version

SANDRA D. FENLEY

Table of Contents

Introduction

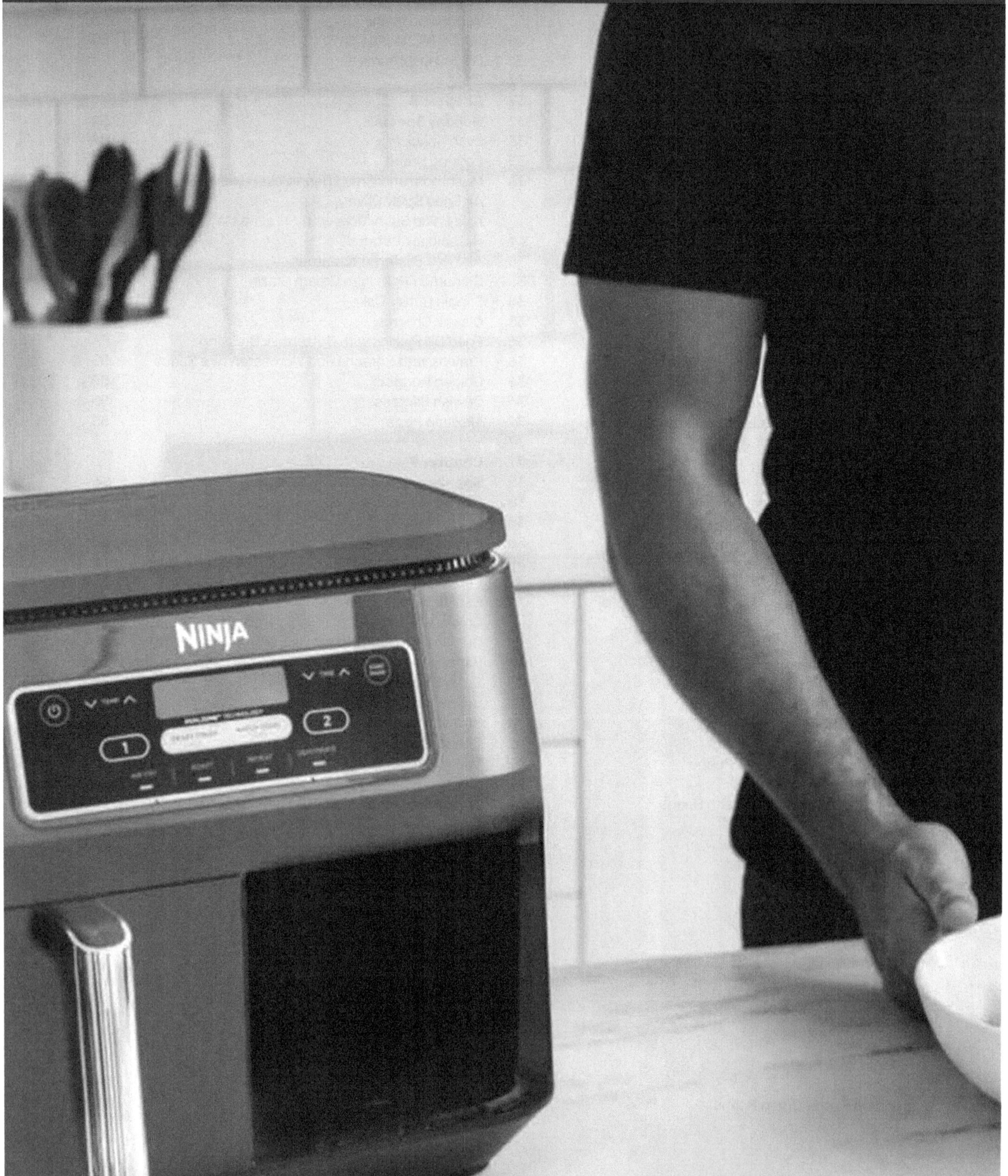

I f you're a fan of fried food, you're in luck. The Ninja Foodi Air Fryer is a tool that can help you enjoy all kinds of fried goodness without the hassle and mess of an actual fryer. Not only is a "Ninja Foodi 2-Basket Air Fryer Cookbook" most advanced air fryer cookbook on the market, but it is also so much more. The ninja is a new way to cook. It combines the convenience of an air fryer with the power of a full-size oven and the flexibility of cooking in various ways. With 900 watts of power and different cooking settings, this machine can handle everything from simple baking to deep-frying. Plus, it's smart enough to know when to turn it off after you're done cooking for safety concerns. This cookbook includes recipes for everything from salads and omelets to burgers and French fries. You'll also find recipes for dishes like lasagna and chicken wings that use both baskets at once! This book also includes some step-by-step guides on preparing your food in the air fryer, as well as tips on getting the most out of your purchase. You won't be able to resist these tasty treats once you try them!

Chapter 1
knowing the Ninja Foodi 2-Basket Air Fryer

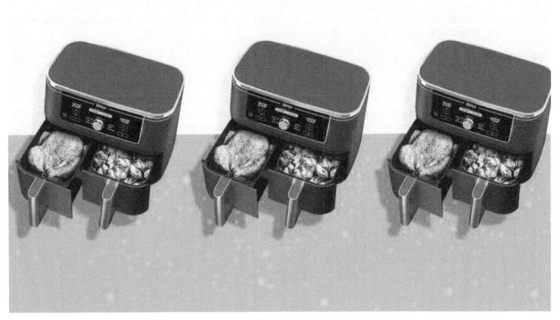

This Ninja Foodi 2-Basket Air Fryer is a small fryer that can cook food quickly and easily. It's perfect for making small batches of fried food. It is powerful and cooks food with minimal oil. It's perfect for making healthier, more flavorful meals at home and is easy to use! The Ninja Foodi 2-Basket Air Fryer uses less than 1/3 of the oil compared to traditional frying. The nonstick cooking basket in this unit allows you to easily remove food from the basket without draining any oil or grease. The Ninja Foodi 2-Basket Air Fryer has an automatic shutoff feature that turns off the unit when it reaches a preset temperature or runs out of power. It also has a brushed stainless steel exterior and interior, which makes it look sleek and modern while also providing durability. It is easy to clean, which means you can use the same unit repeatedly without worrying about whether or not it will hold up over time. The air fryer has two baskets. Each basket holds 3 cups of food at once and can be used separately or together depending on what type of cooking you want with it. The lid fits tightly onto both baskets so they don't fall off during use—which would be extremely inconvenient!

The Ninja Foodi 2-Basket Air Fryer is great for making:

Flatbreads

French fries

Chicken fingers (or any other type of finger food)

How to Use your Ninja

The Ninja Foodi 2-Basket Air Fryer being a handy appliance can help you prepare delicious meals with minimal fuss. It can cook everything from chicken and beef to potatoes, eggs, and vegetables. To use your ninja:

- Plug in your Ninja Foodi 2-Basket Air Fryer for a first time: allow it to warm up for at least 15 minutes.
- Place the basket into the air fryer, and close the lid.
- Select the function, for example, air frying.
- Set your air fryer timer to cook on high heat.
- Once the timer goes off, immediately remove the basket from the air fryer by pushing down one of the handles on either side, then unplugging it from your outlet. Do not attempt to lift or move it in any way—doing so could damage it or cause it to malfunction catastrophically! Allow the food inside to cool completely before removing them from their baskets, as they will be very hot after cooking!

What are the customizable programs on your ninja

AIR BROIL

Air broiling is a great way to cook meat at home. It's also a great way to make healthy meals that are high in protein and low in fat, which means they're good for you! One of the best parts about air broiling is that it doesn't require oil or grease. This means you can use less oil in your cooking, so there's less risk of heart disease and other health problems associated with eating too much fat.

AIR FRY

Air frying works by heating food between two plates above a fan. This creates a convection oven effect, which means that when your food cooks, it does not burn or dry out because the air around it is heated. Air fryers can be used for everything from making French fries to preparing chicken wings or fish filets. You can even use them as a safe way to grill vegetables and meats like steak or chicken breasts without using any oil or butter! Air frying works best when using a Ninja Foodi 2-Basket Air Fryer with temperature settings between 400 degrees F and 425 degrees F (204 degrees C and 216 degrees C).

ROAST

Roasting is one of the easiest ways to cook meat, especially when you want to add some flavor. But if you've ever tried roasting in the oven or on the stovetop, you know there are two problems: it's slow and requires more time than you have. And if your oven doesn't have enough space for all those vegetables, that's another problem! The Ninja Foodi 2-Basket Air Fryer solves all those problems by giving you control over your cooking time and dish size. You can roast chicken or vegetables in just minutes—even while making other dishes, so they don't get cold. And when it comes to serving up big batches of food at once, this air fryer is perfect. You can make 20 pieces of chicken breast at once and then freeze them in individual bags, so they're ready whenever your family wants some tasty grilled chicken!

REHEAT

After cooking, we recommend cooling your food to room temperature before reheating it. The Ninja Foodi 2-Basket Air Fryer is a best way to rapidly reheat food without drying it out. It's fast and easy so that you can prepare your favorite meals with less time and energy. The air fryer heats up quickly and produces evenly cooked food that doesn't burn or stick to the pan, so even the fussiest eaters will love it!

DEHYDRATE

Dehydrating in a Ninja Foodi 2-Basket Air Fryer is a great way to dehydrate foods quickly. It can be used for any food you want to dehydrate and will ensure that the food is done properly so that it does not get burned or misshapen. You will be able to dehydrate fruits, vegetables, nuts, jerky, and more with this air fryer.

BAKE

This Ninja Foodi 2-Basket Air Fryer is the perfect baking companion for making cookies or cakes. This air fryer comes with an adjustable thermostat and an easy-to-read digital screen. You can choose cooking modes. The convection mode cooks at a lower temperature for crispier results, while the bake mode cooks at a higher temperature for softer results.

To start cooking more conveniently, consider buying our Ninja Foodi 2-Basket Air Fryer Cookbook. It's one of the best cookbooks to help you learn how to use your air fryer efficiently and effectively. This book contains recipes that are easy to follow and simple to understand. It also comes with a shopping list so you can easily prepare all the ingredients needed for each recipe. So if you're looking for an easy way to cook healthy meals at home, this is the perfect cookbook! The kitchen is calling!

Cleaning and Caring for Ninja Foodi

2-Basket Air Fryer

Following each use, you must give the device a thorough cleaning. Whenever you want to clean your device, make sure it is unplugged from the wall.

MAIN UNIT

Use a moist cloth to wash the product and the control panel. WARNING: DO NOT SUBMERGE the product in any kind of liquid. Dishwashers should never be used to clean the main unit.

CRISPER PLATES

Both the dishwasher and manual washing are suitable for crisper plates. You may either let everything dry naturally or dry it with a towel if you wash it by hand.

BASKETS

A dishwasher or hand washing is acceptable for these baskets. Dry all components by either letting them air dry or patting them dry with a towel if you're hand washing them. We advise hand washing your basket to ensure its longevity. Put the plates or baskets from the crisper into a sink full of warm, soapy water to loosen any food particles that may be adhered to them.

Ninja Dual Zone Air Fryer Cooking Tips

If you're using the Ninja Air Fryer for the first time, remember to preheat it for 3 minutes at 200°C to eliminate any manufacturing smells.

For frozen foods, preheat the air fryer for 5 minutes at 199°C to ensure that your food cooks evenly.

After the preheating cycle is completed, add your food to the baskets and ensure the food is not touching the sides of the baskets to avoid uneven cooking.

If you wish the cooking in both compartments to finish at the same time (when foods have different temps, times, or cook functions), select the desired cooking function in Zone 1 and Zone 2, press SYNC, and then press the start button to initiate cooking in the zone with the longest cooking time. The other zone will display Hold, and the unit will beep and activate the second zone when both zones have the same time remaining.

If you wish to cook a larger amount of the same food, put ingredients in the baskets and insert them in both zones. Select the desired cooking function, temperature, and time. Press the MATCH button to copy the zone 1 settings to zone 2. Then Press' start' to begin cooking in both zones.

Remove the food using silicone-tipped tongs or utensils.

Frequency Asked Questions & Notes

How do I change the time or temperature if I only use one zone?

When only one zone is on, the up and down arrows can be used to alter the time or temperature at any time.

How do I change the time or temperature when both zones are in use?

Choose the zone you want, then use the arrows next to TEMP to alter the temperature or the arrows next to TIME to change the time.

How do I take a moment or stop one zone once using both zones?

Choose the zone you want to stop or start playing in, and then press this same START/PAUSE button.

When air-frying, why do some ingredients fly around?

From time to time, the air fryer's fan will move light foods around. Use made of wood toothpicks to keep food like the top bread slice on a sandwich from falling off.

Can I air-fry things that are wet and battered?

Yes, but make sure you use the right breading method. It's essential to coat foods with flour, egg, and bread crumbs in that order. So that crumbs don't get blown away by the fan, press the breading firmly onto the battered items.

What caused a circuit breaker to trip while the unit was being used?

The unit utilizes 1690 watts of electrical power, so it needs to be plugged into a 15-amp outlet. If you plug a plug into a 10-amp breaker, the breaker will trip. When the unit is in use, it is also essential that it is the only thing plugged into an outlet. Make sure the unit is the only thing plugged into an outlet on a 15-amp blocker to avoid tripping a breaker.

Helpful Advice for Ninja dual zone air fryer

Make sure the ingredients are laid out evenly and without overlap on the bottom of the drawer for consistent browning. Make careful to shake the ingredients halfway through the designated cooking time if they are overlapping.

You can alter the cooking temperature and duration at any moment.

Simply choose the zone you wish to change, then use the TEMP or TIME arrows to change the temperature or the time.

Reduce the temperature by 10°C if you're converting recipes from your normal oven.

To prevent overcooking, periodically check your food.

On occasion, the air fryer's fan will fling light meals in all directions.

Secure food with cocktail sticks, such as the top slice of bread on a sandwich, to help with this.

For consistent, crisp results, the crisper plates elevate the ingredients in the drawers so that air can circulate under and around them.

Pressing the dial after choosing a cooking function will start cooking right away. The temperature and time settings on the device will be used.

Use at least 1 tablespoon of oil when cooking fresh veggies and potatoes for the best results. To obtain the required level of crispiness, add extra oil as needed.

For the best outcomes, keep an eye on the food while it cooks and take it out when the required level of brownness has been reached. In order to keep track of the interior temperatures of meat and fish, we advise utilising an instant-read thermometer.

To achieve the greatest results, take food out of the oven as soon as the cooking process is finished.

Chapter 2
Dessert Recipes

Apple Hand Pies

Prep Time: 15 minutes | Cook Time: 21 minutes | Serves 8

- 8 tablespoons butter, softened
- 12 tablespoons brown sugar
- 2 teaspoons cinnamon, ground
- 4 medium Granny Smith apples, diced
- 2 teaspoons cornstarch
- 4 teaspoons cold water
- 1 (14-oz) package pastry, 9-inch crust pie
- Cooking spray
- 1 tablespoon grapeseed oil
- ½ cup powdered sugar
- 2 teaspoons milk

1. Toss apples with brown sugar, butter, and cinnamon in a suitable skillet.
2. Place the skillet over medium heat and stir cook for 5 minutes.
3. Mix cornstarch with cold water in a small bowl.
4. Add cornstarch mixture into the apple and cook for 1 minute until it thickens.
5. Remove this filling from the heat and allow it to cool.
6. Unroll the pie crust and spray on a floured surface.
7. Cut the dough into 16 equal rectangles.
8. Wet the edges of the 8 rectangles with water and divide the apple filling at the center of these rectangles.
9. Place the other 8 rectangles on top and crimp the edges with a fork, then make 2-3 slashes on top.
10. Place 4 small pies in each of the crisper plate.
11. Return the crisper plate to the Ninja Foodi Dual Zone Air Fryer.
12. Choose the Air Fry mode for Zone 1 and set the temperature to 390 degrees F/ 200 degrees C and the time to 17 minutes.
13. Select the "MATCH" button to copy the settings for Zone 2.
14. Initiate cooking by pressing the START/STOP button.
15. Flip the pies once cooked halfway through, and resume cooking.
16. Meanwhile, mix sugar with milk.
17. Pour this mixture over the apple pies.
18. Serve fresh.

Chicken Cordon Bleu

Prep Time: 5 minutes | Cook Time: 16 Minutes | Serves 2

- 2 boneless, skinless chicken breasts
- ¼ teaspoon salt
- 2 teaspoons Dijon mustard
- 2 ounces deli ham
- 2 ounces Swiss, fontina, or Gruyère cheese
- ⅓ cup all-purpose flour
- 1 egg
- ½ cup breadcrumbs

1. Pat the chicken breasts with a paper towel. Season the chicken with the salt. Pound the chicken breasts to 1½ inches thick. Create a pouch by slicing the side of each chicken breast. Spread 1 teaspoon Dijon mustard inside the pouch of each chicken breast. Wrap a 1-ounce slice of ham around a 1-ounce slice of cheese and place into the pouch. Repeat with the remaining ham and cheese.
2. In a medium bowl, place the flour.
3. In a second bowl, whisk the egg.
4. In a third bowl, place the breadcrumbs.
5. Dredge the chicken in the flour and shake off the excess. Next, dip the chicken into the egg and then in the breadcrumbs. Set the chicken on a plate and repeat with the remaining chicken piece.
6. Preheat the air fryer to 360°F.
7. Place the chicken in the air fryer basket and spray liberally with cooking spray. Cook for 8 minutes, turn the chicken breasts over, and liberally spray with cooking spray again; cook another 6 minutes. Once golden brown, check for an internal temperature of 165°F.

Japanese-style Turkey Meatballs
Prep Time: 15 minutes | Cook Time: 25 Minutes| Serves 4

- 1 1/3 lb ground turkey
- ¼ cup panko bread crumbs
- 4 chopped scallions
- ¼ cup chopped cilantro
- 1 egg
- 1 tbsp grated ginger
- 1 garlic clove, minced
- 3 tbsp shoyu
- 2 tsp toasted sesame oil
- ¾ tsp salt
- 2 tbsp oyster sauce sauce
- 2 tbsp fresh orange juice

1. Add ground turkey, panko, 3 scallions, cilantro, egg, ginger, garlic, 1 tbsp of shoyu sauce, sesame oil, and salt in a bowl. Mix with hands until combined. Divide the mixture into 12 equal parts and roll into balls. Preheat air fryer to 380°F. Place the meatballs in the greased frying basket. Bake for about 9-11 minutes, flipping once until browned and cooked through. Repeat for all meatballs.
2. In a small saucepan over medium heat, add oyster sauce, orange juice and remaining shoyu sauce. Bring to a boil, then reduce the heat to low. Cook until the sauce is slightly reduced, 3 minutes. Serve the meatballs with the oyster sauce drizzled over them and topped with the remaining scallions.

Pulled Turkey Quesadillas
Prep Time: 5 minutes | Cook Time: 15 Minutes | Serves 4

- ¾ cup pulled cooked turkey breast
- 6 tortilla wraps
- 1/3 cup grated Swiss cheese
- 1 small red onion, sliced
- 2 tbsp Mexican chili sauce

1. Preheat air fryer to 400°F.
2. Lay 3 tortilla wraps on a clean workspace, then spoon equal amounts of Swiss cheese, turkey, Mexican chili sauce, and red onion on the tortillas.
3. Spritz the exterior of the tortillas with cooking spray.
4. Air Fry the quesadillas, one at a time, for 5-8 minutes.
5. The cheese should be melted and the outsides crispy. Serve.

Za'atar Chicken Drumsticks

Prep Time: 5 minutes | Cook Time: 45 Minutes| Serves 4

- 2 tbsp butter, melted
- 8 chicken drumsticks
- 1 ½ tbsp Za'atar seasoning
- Salt and pepper to taste
- 1 lemon, zested
- 2 tbsp parsley, chopped

1. Preheat air fryer to 390°F.
2. Mix the Za'atar seasoning, lemon zest, parsley, salt, and pepper in a bowl.
3. Add the chicken drumsticks and toss to coat.
4. Place them in the air fryer and brush them with butter.
5. Air Fry for 18-20 minutes, flipping once until crispy.
6. Serve and enjoy!

Crispy Chicken Tenders

Prep Time: 5 minutes | Cook Time: 20 Minutes | Serves 4

- 1 egg
- ¼ cup almond milk
- ¼ cup almond flour
- ¼ cup bread crumbs
- Salt and pepper to taste
- ½ tsp dried thyme
- ½ tsp dried sage
- ½ tsp garlic powder
- ½ tsp chili powder
- 1 lb chicken tenderloins
- 1 lemon, quartered

1. Preheat air fryer to 360°F.
2. Whisk together the egg and almond milk in a bowl until frothy.
3. Mix the flour, bread crumbs, salt, pepper, thyme, sage, chili powder and garlic powder in a separate bowl.
4. Dip each chicken tenderloin into the egg mixture, then coat with the bread crumb mixture.
5. Put the breaded chicken tenderloins into the frying basket in a single layer.
6. Air Fry for 12 minutes, turning once.
7. Serve with lemon slices.

Taquitos

Prep Time: 5 minutes | Cook Time: 6 Minutes Per Batch | Serves 12

- 1 teaspoon butter
- 2 tablespoons chopped green onions
- 1 cup cooked chicken, shredded
- 2 tablespoons chopped green chiles
- 2 ounces Pepper Jack cheese, shredded
- 4 tablespoons salsa
- ½ teaspoon lime juice
- ¼ teaspoon cumin
- ½ teaspoon chile powder
- ⅛ teaspoon garlic powder
- 12 corn tortillas
- oil for misting or cooking spray

1. Melt butter in a saucepan over medium heat. Add green onions and sauté a minute or two, until tender.
2. Remove from heat and stir in the chicken, green chiles, cheese, salsa, lime juice, and seasonings.
3. Preheat air fryer to 390°F.
4. To soften refrigerated tortillas, wrap in damp paper towels and microwave for 30 to 60 seconds, until slightly warmed.
5. Remove one tortilla at a time, keeping others covered with the damp paper towels. Place a heaping tablespoon of filling into tortilla, roll up and secure with toothpick. Spray all sides with oil or cooking spray.
6. Place taquitos in air fryer basket, either in a single layer or stacked. To stack, leave plenty of space between taquitos and alternate the direction of the layers, 4 on the bottom lengthwise, then 4 more on top crosswise.
7. Cook for 6minutes or until brown and crispy.
8. Repeat steps 6 and 7 to cook remaining taquitos.
9. Serve hot with guacamole, sour cream, salsa or all three!

Walnuts Fritters

Prep Time: 15 minutes | Cook Time: 15 minutes| Serves 6

- 1 cup all-purpose flour
- ½ cup walnuts, chopped
- ¼ cup white sugar
- ¼ cup milk
- 1 egg
- 1 ½ teaspoons baking powder
- 1 pinch salt
- Cooking spray
- 2 tablespoons white sugar
- ½ teaspoon ground cinnamon
- ½ cup confectioners› sugar
- 1 tablespoon milk
- ½ teaspoon caramel extract
- ¼ teaspoons ground cinnamon

1. Layer both crisper plate with parchment paper.
2. Grease the parchment paper with cooking spray.
3. Whisk flour with milk, ¼ cup of sugar, egg, baking powder, and salt in a small bowl.
4. Separately mix 2 tablespoons of sugar with cinnamon in another bowl, toss in walnuts and mix well to coat.
5. Stir in flour mixture and mix until combined.
6. Drop the fritters mixture using a cookie scoop into the two crisper plate.
7. Return the crisper plate to the Ninja Foodi Dual Zone Air Fryer.
8. Choose the Air Fry mode for Zone 1 and set the temperature to 375 degrees F/ 190 degrees C and the time to 15 minutes.
9. Select the "MATCH" button to copy the settings for Zone 2.
10. Initiate cooking by pressing the START/STOP button.
11. Flip the fritters once cooked halfway through, then resume cooking.
12. Meanwhile, whisk milk, caramel extract, confectioners' sugar, and cinnamon in a bowl.
13. Transfer fritters to a wire rack and allow them to cool.
14. Drizzle with a glaze over the fritters.

Air-fried Turkey Breast With Cherry Glaze

Prep Time: 5 minutes | Cook Time: 54 Minutes | Serves 6

- 1 (5-pound) turkey breast
- 2 teaspoons olive oil
- 1 teaspoon dried thyme
- ½ teaspoon dried sage
- 1 teaspoon salt
- ½ teaspoon freshly ground black pepper
- ½ cup cherry preserves
- 1 tablespoon chopped fresh thyme leaves
- 1 teaspoon soy sauce
- freshly ground black pepper

1. All turkeys are built differently, so depending on the turkey breast and how your butcher has prepared it, you may need to trim the bottom of the ribs in order to get the turkey to sit upright in the air fryer basket without touching the heating element. The key to this recipe is getting the right size turkey breast. Once you've managed that, the rest is easy, so make sure your turkey breast fits into the air fryer basket before you Preheat the air fryer.
2. Preheat the air fryer to 350°F.
3. Brush the turkey breast all over with the olive oil. Combine the thyme, sage, salt and pepper and rub the outside of the turkey breast with the spice mixture.
4. Transfer the seasoned turkey breast to the air fryer basket, breast side up, and air-fry at 350°F for 25 minutes. Turn the turkey breast on its side and air-fry for another 12 minutes. Turn the turkey breast on the opposite side and air-fry for 12 more minutes. The internal temperature of the turkey breast should reach 165°F when fully cooked.
5. While the turkey is air-frying, make the glaze by combining the cherry preserves, fresh thyme, soy sauce and pepper in a small bowl. When the cooking time is up, return the turkey breast to an upright position and brush the glaze all over the turkey. Air-fry for a final 5 minutes, until the skin is nicely browned and crispy. Let the turkey rest, loosely tented with foil, for at least 5 minutes before slicing and serving.

Windsor's Chicken Salad

Prep Time: 5 minutes | Cook Time: 30 Minutes| Serves 4

- ½ cup halved seedless red grapes
- 2 chicken breasts, cubed
- Salt and pepper to taste
- ¾ cup mayonnaise
- 1 tbsp lemon juice
- 2 tbsp chopped parsley
- ½ cup chopped celery
- 1 shallot, diced

1. Preheat air fryer to 350°F.
2. Sprinkle chicken with salt and pepper.
3. Place the chicken cubes in the frying basket and Air Fry for 9 minutes, flipping once.
4. In a salad bowl, combine the cooked chicken, mayonnaise, lemon juice, parsley, grapes, celery, and shallot and let chill covered in the fridge for 1 hour up to overnight.

Chicken Breast Burgers

Prep Time: 5 minutes | Cook Time: 35 Minutes| Serves 4

- 2 chicken breasts
- 1 cup dill pickle juice
- 1 cup buttermilk
- 1 egg
- ½ cup flour
- Salt and pepper to taste
- 4 buns
- 2 pickles, sliced

1. Cut the chicken into cutlets by cutting them in half horizontally on a cutting board. Transfer them to a large bowl along with pickle juice and ½ cup of buttermilk. Toss to coat, then marinate for 30 minutes in the fridge.
2. Preheat air fryer to 370°F. In a shallow bowl, beat the egg and the rest of the buttermilk to combine. In another shallow bowl, mix flour, salt, and pepper. Dip the marinated cutlet in the egg mixture, then dredge in flour. Place the cutlets in the greased frying basket and Air Fry for 12 minutes, flipping once halfway through. Remove the cutlets and pickles on buns and serve.

Chapter 3
Breakfast Recipes

Eggs in Avocado Cups

Prep Time: 15 minutes | Cook Time: 12 minutes | Serves 4

- 2 avocados, halved and pitted
- 4 eggs
- Salt and ground black pepper, as required

1. Line each basket of "Zone 1" and "Zone 2" of Ninja Foodi 2-Basket Air Fryer with a greased square piece of foil.
2. Press "Zone 1" and "Zone 2" and then rotate the knob for each zone to select "Bake".
3. Set the temperature to 390 degrees F/ 200 degrees C for both zones and then set the time for 5 minutes to preheat.
4. Meanwhile, carefully scoop out about 2 teaspoons of flesh from each avocado half.
5. Crack 1 egg in each avocado half and sprinkle with salt and black pepper.
6. After preheating, arrange 2 avocado halves into the basket of each zone.
7. Slide the baskets into Air Fryer and set the time for 12 minutes.
8. After cooking time is completed, transfer the avocado halves and onto serving plates and serve hot.

Scotch Eggs

Prep Time: 10 minutes|Cook Time: 15 minutes|Serves 6

- 1-pound pork sausage
- Salt and pepper to taste
- 6 large hard-boiled eggs
- 1 large egg, lightly beaten
- ¾ cup crushed cornflakes

1. Flatten the sausage into 6 chunks and make a patty to surround each egg. Season with salt and pepper.
2. Roll in cornflakes crumbs, then in beaten egg.
3. Press "Zone 1" and "Zone 2" and then rotate the knob for each zone to select "Bake".
4. Set the temperature to 400 degrees F/ 200 degrees C for both zones, and then set the time for 5 minutes to preheat.
5. After preheating, spray the Air-Fryer basket of each zone with cooking spray, line them with parchment paper, and place eggs.
6. Slide them into Air Fryer and set the time for 14 minutes.
7. After cooking time is completed, transfer them onto serving plates and serve hot.

Breakfast Sweet Potato Skins

Prep Time: 10 minutes| Cook Time: 25 minutes| Serves 4

- 2 medium sweet potatoes
- 2 tsp. olive oil
- 4 eggs
- ¼ cup whole milk
- Salt and pepper
- 4 slices of cooked bacon

1. Wash the sweet potatoes and chop them into three or four pieces. Microwave for 6-8 minutes, or until soft, depending on their size.
2. Cut the potatoes in half lengthwise. Remove the potato flesh with a ¼-inch border around the edges. Save the sweet potato that has been scooped for another use.
3. Brush the skins of the potatoes with olive oil and season with salt.
4. Press "Zone 1" and "Zone 2" and then rotate the knob for each zone to select "Bake".
5. Set the temperature to 400 degrees F/ 200 degrees C for both zones, and then set the time for 5 minutes to preheat.
6. After preheating, spray the Air-Fryer basket of each zone with cooking spray, line them with parchment paper, and arrange potato skins.
7. Slide them into Air Fryer and set the time for 10 minutes.
8. In a nonstick skillet, whisk the eggs, milk, salt, and pepper. Cook, stirring, until there are no visible liquid eggs in the mixture over medium heat.
9. Add ¼ of the scrambled eggs and 1 slice of crumbled bacon on top of each potato skin when cooked.
10. Return to the Air Fryer basket and cook for 3 minutes at 400 degrees F/ 200 degrees C.
11. After cooking time is completed, transfer them onto serving plates and serve hot.

Green Salad with Crispy Fried Goat Cheese and Baked Croutons

Prep time: 10 minutes, plus 5 minutes to cool|Cook time: 10 minutes |Serves 4

FOR THE GOAT CHEESE

- 1 (4-ounce) log soft goat cheese
- ½ cup panko bread crumbs
- 2 tablespoons vegetable oil
- FOR THE CROUTONS
- 2 slices Italian-style sandwich bread
- 2 tablespoons vegetable oil
- 1 tablespoon poultry seasoning
- ½ teaspoon kosher salt
- ¼ teaspoon freshly ground black pepper

FOR THE SALAD

- 8 cups green leaf lettuce leaves
- ½ cup store-bought balsamic vinaigrette

TO PREP THE GOAT CHEESE:

1. Cut the goat cheese into 8 round slices.
2. Spread the panko on a plate. Gently press the cheese into the panko to coat on both sides. Drizzle with the oil.

To prep the croutons: Cut the bread into cubes and place them in a large bowl. Add the oil, poultry seasoning, salt, and black pepper. Mix well to coat the bread cubes evenly.

TO COOK THE GOAT CHEESE AND CROUTONS:

1. Install a crisper plate in each of the two baskets. Place the goat cheese in the Zone 1 basket and insert the basket in the unit. Place the croutons in the Zone 2 basket and insert the basket in the unit.
2. Select Zone 1, select AIR FRY, set the temperature to 400°F, and set the timer to 6 minutes.
3. Select Zone 2, select BAKE, set the temperature to 390°F, and set the timer to 10 minutes. Select SMART FINISH.
4. Press START/PAUSE to begin cooking.
5. When cooking is complete, the goat cheese will be golden brown and the croutons crisp.
6. Remove the Zone 1 basket. Let the goat cheese cool in the basket for 5 minutes; it will firm up as it cools.

To assemble the salad: In a large bowl, combine the lettuce, vinaigrette, and croutons. Toss well. Divide the salad among four plates. Top each plate with 2 pieces of goat cheese.

Breakfast Cookies

Prep Time: 20 minutes | Cook Time: 10 minutes| Serves 6

- 1 cup mashed ripe bananas
- ½ cup chunky peanut butter
- ½ cup honey
- 1 teaspoon vanilla extract
- 1 cup oats
- ½ cup whole wheat flour
- ¼ cup nonfat dry milk powder
- 2 teaspoons ground cinnamon
- ½ teaspoon salt
- ¼ teaspoon baking soda
- 1 cup dried cranberries

1. Blend the banana, peanut butter, honey, and vanilla until smooth.
2. Combine oats, flour, milk powder, cinnamon, salt, and baking soda in a separate dish; gradually stir into the banana mixture. Add the dried cranberries and mix well.
3. Press "Zone 1" and "Zone 2" and then rotate the knob for each zone to select "Air Fry".
4. Set the temperature to 300 degrees F/ 150 degrees C for both zones, and then set the time for 5 minutes to preheat.
5. After preheating, spray the Air-Fryer basket of each zone with cooking spray, line them with parchment paper, and drop dough by ¼ cupful 2 inches apart in batches.
6. Slide the basket into Air Fryer and set the time for 8 minutes.
7. After cooking time is completed, transfer them onto serving plates and serve hot.

Egg and Veggies Croquettes

Prep Time: 30 minutes| Cook Time: 15 minutes |Serves 6

- 3 tablespoons butter
- 3 tablespoons all-purpose flour
- ¾ cup 2% milk
- 6 large hard-boiled eggs, chopped
- ½ cup chopped fresh asparagus
- ½ cup chopped green onions
- ⅓ cup shredded cheddar cheese
- 1 tablespoon minced fresh tarragon
- ¼ teaspoon salt
- ¼ teaspoon pepper
- 1-¾ cups panko bread crumbs
- 3 large eggs, beaten
- Cooking spray

1. Melt butter in a large pot over medium heat. Cook and stir until gently browned, about 1-2 minutes after adding the flour. Gradually whisk in the milk, then boil and stir until the sauce has thickened.
2. Add hard-boiled eggs, asparagus, green onions, cheese, tarragon, salt, and pepper and mix. Refrigerate for at least 2 hours before serving.
3. Shape ¼ cupful of egg mixture into long ovals. Separate the bread crumbs and eggs into shallow dishes.
4. To coat the logs, roll them in crumbs, dip them in egg and roll them in crumbs again, patting to help the coating cling.
5. Press "Zone 1" and "Zone 2" and then rotate the knob for each zone to select "Air Fry".
6. Set the temperature to 350 degrees F/ 175 degrees C for both zones, and then set the time for 5 minutes to preheat.
7. After preheating, spray the Air-Fryer basket of each zone with cooking spray, line them with parchment paper, and croquettes in a single layer. Spritz with cooking spray.
8. Slide them into Air Fryer and set the time for 10 minutes. Turn them and again spritz cooking spray and cook 4 minutes longer.
9. After cooking time is completed, transfer them onto serving plates and serve hot.

Ham and Egg Pockets

Prep Time: 20 minutes | Cook Time: 10 minutes | Serves 6

- 1 large egg
- 2 teaspoons 2% milk
- 2 teaspoons butter
- 1 ounce thinly sliced ham, chopped
- 2 tablespoons shredded cheddar cheese
- 4 ounces refrigerated crescent rolls

1. Combine the egg and milk in a small bowl. Heat the butter in a small skillet until it is melted.
2. Cook and whisk the egg mixture over medium heat until the eggs are set. Turn off the heat. Combine the ham and cheese in a mixing bowl.
3. Make two rectangles out of crescent dough. Spoon half the filling down the center of each rectangle. Fold dough over filling; pinch to seal.
4. Press "Zone 1" and "Zone 2" and then rotate the knob for each zone to select "Air Fry".
5. Set the temperature to 300 degrees F/ 150 degrees C for both zones, and then set the time for 5 minutes to preheat.
6. After preheating, spray the Air-Fryer basket of each zone with cooking spray, line them with parchment paper, and place them.
7. Slide the basket into Air Fryer and set the time for 10 minutes.
8. After cooking time is completed, transfer them onto serving plates and serve hot.

Potato and Parsnip Latkes with Baked Apples

Prep time: 20 minutes, plus 5 minutes to sit|Cook time: 20 minutes |Serves 4

FOR THE LATKES

- 2 medium russet potatoes, peeled
- 1 large egg white
- 2 tablespoons all-purpose flour
- ¼ teaspoon garlic powder
- ¼ teaspoon kosher salt
- ¼ teaspoon freshly ground black pepper
- 1 medium parsnip, peeled and shredded
- 2 scallions, thinly sliced
- 2 tablespoons vegetable oil
- FOR THE BAKED APPLES
- 2 Golden Delicious apples, peeled and diced
- 2 tablespoons granulated sugar
- 2 teaspoons unsalted butter, cut into small pieces

TO PREP THE LATKES:

1. Grate the potatoes using the large holes of a box grater. Squeeze as much liquid out of the potatoes as you can into a large bowl. Set the potatoes aside in a separate bowl.
2. Let the potato liquid sit for 5 minutes, during which time the potato starch will settle to the bottom of the bowl. Pour off the water that has risen to the top, leaving the potato starch in the bowl.
3. Add the egg white, flour, salt, and black pepper to the potato starch to form a thick paste. Add the potatoes, parsnip, and scallions and mix well. Divide the mixture into 4 patties. Brush both sides of each patty with the oil.

To prep the baked apples: Place the apples in the Zone 2 basket. Sprinkle the sugar and butter over the top.

TO COOK THE LATKES AND APPLES:

1. Install a crisper plate in the Zone 1 basket. Place the latkes in the basket in a single layer, then insert the basket in the unit. Insert the Zone 2 basket in the unit.
2. Select Zone 1, select AIR FRY, set the temperature to 375°F, and set the timer to 15 minutes.
3. Select Zone 2, select BAKE, set the temperature to 330°F, and set the timer to 20 minutes. Select SMART FINISH.
4. Press START/PAUSE to begin cooking.
5. When both timers read 5 minutes, press START/ PAUSE. Remove the Zone 1 basket and use silicone-tipped tongs or a spatula to flip the latkes. Reinsert the basket in the unit. Remove the Zone 2 basket and gently mash the apples with a fork or the back of a spoon. Reinsert the basket and press START/ PAUSE to resume cooking.
6. When cooking is complete, the latkes should be golden brown and cooked through and the apples very soft.
7. Transfer the latkes to a plate and serve with apples on the side.

Caprese Panini with Zucchini Chips

Prep time: 20 minutes|Cook time: 20 minutes |Serves 4

FOR THE PANINI

- 4 tablespoons pesto
- 8 slices Italian-style sandwich bread
- 1 tomato, diced
- 6 ounces fresh mozzarella cheese, shredded
- ¼ cup mayonnaise
- FOR THE ZUCCHINI CHIPS
- ½ cup all-purpose flour
- 2 large eggs
- ¼ teaspoon freshly ground black pepper
- ⅛ teaspoon kosher salt
- ½ cup panko bread crumbs
- ¼ cup grated Parmesan cheese
- 1 teaspoon Italian seasoning
- 1 medium zucchini, cut into ¼-inch-thick rounds
- 2 tablespoons vegetable oil

TO PREP THE PANINI:

1. Spread 1 tablespoon of pesto each on 4 slices of the bread. Layer the diced tomato and shredded mozzarella on the other 4 slices of bread. Top the tomato/cheese mixture with the pesto-coated bread, pesto-side down, to form 4 sandwiches.
2. Spread the outside of each sandwich (both bread slices) with a thin layer of the mayonnaise.

TO PREP THE ZUCCHINI CHIPS:

1. Set up a breading station with three small shallow bowls. Place the flour in the first bowl. In the second bowl, beat together the eggs, salt, and black pepper. Place the panko, Parmesan, and Italian seasoning in the third bowl.
2. Bread the zucchini in this order: First, dip the slices into the flour, coating both sides. Then, dip into the beaten egg. Finally, coat in the panko mixture. Drizzle the zucchini on both sides with the oil.

TO COOK THE PANINI AND ZUCCHINI CHIPS:

1. Install a crisper plate in each of the two baskets. Place 2 sandwiches in the Zone 1 basket and insert the basket in the unit. Place half of the zucchini chips in a single layer in the Zone 2 basket and insert the basket in the unit.
2. Select Zone 1, select AIR FRY, set the temperature to 375°F, and set the timer to 20 minutes.
3. Select Zone 2, select AIR FRY, set the temperature to 400°F, and set the timer to 20 minutes. Select SMART FINISH.
4. Press START/PAUSE to begin cooking.
5. When the Zone 1 timer reads 15 minutes, press START/PAUSE. Remove the basket, and use silicone-tipped tongs or a spatula to flip the sandwiches. Reinsert the basket and press START/PAUSE to resume cooking.
6. When both timers read 10 minutes, press START/PAUSE. Remove the Zone 1 basket and transfer the sandwiches to a plate. Place the remaining 2 sandwiches into the basket and insert the basket in the unit. Remove the Zone 2 basket and transfer the zucchini chips to a serving plate. Place the remaining zucchini chips in the basket. Reinsert the basket and press START/PAUSE to resume cooking.
7. When the Zone 1 timer reads 5 minutes, press START/PAUSE. Remove the basket and flip the sandwiches. Reinsert the basket and press START/PAUSE to resume cooking.
8. When cooking is complete, the panini should be toasted and the zucchini chips golden brown and crisp.
9. Cut each panini in half. Serve hot with zucchini chips on the side.

Bacon Cinnamon Rolls

Prep Time: 20 minutes | Cook Time: 10 minutes | Serves 8

- 8 bacon strips
- ¾ cup bourbon
- 1 tube (12.4 ounces) refrigerated cinnamon rolls with icing
- ½ cup chopped pecans
- 2 tablespoons maple syrup

1. In a small bowl, combine the bacon and the bourbon. Refrigerate overnight after sealing. Remove the bacon and pat it dry; toss out the bourbon.
2. Cook bacon in batches in a large skillet over medium heat until nearly crisp but still flexible. Remove to a plate lined with paper towels to drain.
3. Separate the dough into 8 rolls and set aside the frosting packet. Spiral rolls should be unrolled into long strips.
4. Place 1 bacon strip on each dough strip, cut as necessary, and reroll to form a spiral. To seal the ends, pinch them together.
5. Press "Zone 1" and "Zone 2" and then rotate the knob for each zone to select "Air Fry".
6. Set the temperature to 350 degrees F/ 175 degrees C for both zones, and then set the time for 5 minutes to preheat.
7. After preheating, spray the Air-Fryer basket of each zone with cooking spray, line them with parchment paper, and place rolls.
8. Slide the basket into Air Fryer and set the time for 5 minutes.
9. Turn the rolls over and cook for another 4 minutes, or until golden brown.
10. Meanwhile, combine the pecans and maple syrup in a mixing bowl. In a separate bowl, combine the contents of the icing packet.
11. Heat the remaining bacon drippings in the same skillet over medium heat. Cook, stirring regularly until the pecan mixture is gently browned, about 2-3 minutes.
12. After cooking time is completed, transfer them onto serving plates and drizzle half the icing over warm cinnamon rolls; top with half the pecans.

Bacon & Spinach Cups

Prep Time: 15 minutes | Cook Time: 19 minutes | Serves 6

- 6 eggs
- 12 bacon slices, chopped
- 4 cups fresh baby spinach
- ¾ cup heavy cream
- 6 tablespoons Parmesan cheese, grated
- Salt and ground black pepper, as required

1. Heat a non-stick skillet over medium-high heat and cook the bacon for about 6-8 minutes.
2. Add the spinach and cook for about 2-3 minutes.
3. Stir in the heavy cream and Parmesan cheese and cook for about 2-3 minutes.
4. Remove from the heat and set aside to cool slightly.
5. Press "Zone 1" and "Zone 2" of Ninja Foodi 2-Basket Air Fryer and then rotate the knob for each zone to select "Air Fry".
6. Set the temperature to 350 degrees F/ 175 degrees C for both zones and then set the time for 5 minutes to preheat.
7. Crack 1 egg in each of 6 greased ramekins and top with bacon mixture.
8. After preheating, arrange 3 ramekins into the basket of each zone.
9. Slide each basket into Air Fryer and set the time for 5 minutes.
10. After cooking time is completed, remove the ramekins from Air Fryer.
11. Sprinkle the top of each cup with salt and black pepper and serve hot.

Jerk Tofu with Roasted Cabbage

Prep time: 10 minutes, plus 15 minutes to marinate| Cook time: 20 minutes| Serves 4

- FOR THE JERK TOFU
- 1 (14-ounce) package extra-firm tofu, drained
- 1 tablespoon apple cider vinegar
- 1 tablespoon reduced-sodium soy sauce
- 2 tablespoons jerk seasoning
- Juice of 1 lime
- ½ teaspoon kosher salt
- 2 tablespoons olive oil
- FOR THE CABBAGE
- 1 (14-ounce) bag coleslaw mix
- 1 red bell pepper, thinly sliced
- 2 scallions, thinly sliced
- 2 tablespoons water
- 3 garlic cloves, minced
- ¼ teaspoon fresh thyme leaves
- ¼ teaspoon onion powder
- ¼ teaspoon kosher salt
- ¼ teaspoon freshly ground black pepper

TO PREP THE JERK TOFU:

1. Cut the tofu horizontally into 4 slabs.
2. In a shallow dish (big enough to hold the tofu slabs), whisk together the vinegar, soy sauce, jerk seasoning, lime juice, and salt.
3. Place the tofu in the marinade and turn to coat both sides. Cover and marinate for at least 15 minutes (or up to overnight in the refrigerator).

To prep the cabbage: In the Zone 2 basket, combine the coleslaw, bell pepper, scallions, water, garlic, thyme, onion powder, salt, and black pepper.

TO COOK THE TOFU AND CABBAGE:

1. Install a crisper plate in the Zone 1 basket and add the tofu in a single layer. Brush the tofu with the oil and insert the basket in the unit. Insert the Zone 2 basket in the unit.
2. Select Zone 1, select AIR FRY, set the temperature to 390°F, and set the timer to 15 minutes.
3. Select Zone 2, select ROAST, set the temperature to 330°F, and set the timer to 20 minutes. Select SMART FINISH.
4. Press START/PAUSE to begin cooking.
5. When both timers read 5 minutes, press START/PAUSE. Remove the Zone 1 basket and use silicone-tipped tongs to flip the tofu. Reinsert the basket in the unit. Remove the Zone 2 basket and stir the cabbage. Reinsert the basket and press START/PAUSE to resume cooking.
6. When cooking is complete, the tofu will be crispy and browned around the edges and the cabbage soft.
7. Transfer the tofu to four plates and serve with the cabbage on the side.

Savory Soufflé
Prep Time: 15 minutes| Cook Time: 8 minutes| Serves 4

- 4 tablespoons light cream
- 4 eggs
- 2 tablespoons fresh parsley, chopped
- 2 fresh red chilies pepper, chopped
- Salt, as required

1. In a bowl, add all the ingredients and beat until well combined.
2. Divide the mixture into 4 greased soufflé dishes.
3. Press "Zone 1" and "Zone 2" of Ninja Foodi 2-Basket Air Fryer and then rotate the knob for each zone to select "Air Fry".
4. Set the temperature to 390 degrees F/ 200 degrees C for both zones and then set the time for 5 minutes to preheat.
5. After preheating, arrange 2 soufflé dishes into the basket of each zone.
6. Slide each basket into Air Fryer and set the time for 8 minutes.
7. After cooking time is completed, remove the soufflé dishes from Air Fryer and serve warm.

Buffalo Seitan with Crispy Zucchini Noodles
Prep time: 15 minutes |Cook time: 12 minutes |Serves 4

FOR THE BUFFALO SEITAN
- 1 (8-ounce) package precooked seitan strips
- 1 teaspoon garlic powder, divided
- ½ teaspoon onion powder
- ¼ teaspoon smoked paprika
- ¼ cup Louisiana-style hot sauce
- 2 tablespoons vegetable oil
- 1 tablespoon tomato paste
- ¼ teaspoon freshly ground black pepper
- 3 large egg whites
- 1¼ cups all-purpose flour
- 1 teaspoon kosher salt, divided
- 12 ounces seltzer water or club soda
- 5 ounces zucchini noodles
- Nonstick cooking spray

TO PREP THE BUFFALO SEITAN:
1. Season the seitan strips with ½ teaspoon of garlic powder, the onion powder, and smoked paprika.
2. In a large bowl, whisk together the hot sauce, oil, tomato paste, remaining ½ teaspoon of garlic powder, and the black pepper. Set the bowl of Buffalo sauce aside.

TO PREP THE ZUCCHINI NOODLES:
1. In a medium bowl, use a handheld mixer to beat the egg whites until stiff peaks form.
2. In a large bowl, combine the flour and ½ teaspoon of salt. Mix in the seltzer to form a thin batter. Fold in the beaten egg whites.
3. Add the zucchini to the batter and gently mix to coat.

TO COOK THE SEITAN AND ZUCCHINI NOODLES:
1. Install a crisper plate in each of the two baskets. Place the seitan in the Zone 1 basket and insert the basket in the unit. Lift the noodles from the batter one at a time, letting the excess drip off, and place them in the Zone 2 basket. Insert the basket in the unit.
2. Select Zone 1, select BAKE, set the temperature to 370°F, and set the timer to 12 minutes.
3. Select Zone 2, select AIR FRY, set the temperature to 400°F, and set the timer to 12 minutes. Select SMART FINISH.
4. Press START/PAUSE to begin cooking.
5. When the Zone 1 timer reads 2 minutes, press START/PAUSE. Remove the basket and transfer the seitan to the bowl of Buffalo sauce. Turn to coat, then return the seitan to the basket. Reinsert the basket and press START/PAUSE to resume cooking.
6. When cooking is complete, the seitan should be warmed through and the zucchini noodles crisp and light golden brown.
7. Sprinkle the zucchini noodles with the remaining ½ teaspoon of salt. If desired, drizzle extra Buffalo sauce over the seitan. Serve hot.

Balsamic-Glazed Tofu with Roasted Butternut Squash

Prep time: 10 minutes, plus 20 minutes to marinate|Cook time: 40 minutes |Serves 4

FOR THE BALSAMIC TOFU

- 2 tablespoons balsamic vinegar
- 1 tablespoon maple syrup
- 1 teaspoon soy sauce
- 1 teaspoon Dijon mustard
- 1 (14-ounce) package firm tofu, drained and cut into large cubes
- 1 tablespoon canola oil
- FOR THE BUTTERNUT SQUASH
- 1 small butternut squash
- 1 tablespoon canola oil
- 1 teaspoon light brown sugar
- ¼ teaspoon kosher salt
- ¼ teaspoon freshly ground black pepper
- prep the balsamic tofu: In a large bowl, whisk together the vinegar, maple syrup, soy sauce, and mustard. Add the tofu and stir to coat. Cover and marinate for at least 20 minutes (or up to overnight in the refrigerator).

TO PREP THE BUTTERNUT SQUASH:

1. Peel the squash and cut in half lengthwise. Remove and discard the seeds. Cut the squash crosswise into ½-inch-thick slices.
2. Brush the squash pieces with the oil, then sprinkle with the brown sugar, salt, and black pepper.

TO COOK THE TOFU AND SQUASH:

1. Install a crisper plate in each of the two baskets. Place the tofu in the Zone 1 basket, drizzle with the oil, and insert the basket in the unit. Place the squash in the Zone 2 basket and insert the basket in the unit.
2. Select Zone 1, select AIR FRY, set the temperature to 400°F, and set the timer to 10 minutes.
3. Select Zone 2, select ROAST, set the temperature to 400°F, and set the timer to 40 minutes. Select SMART FINISH.
4. Press START/PAUSE to begin cooking.
5. When cooking is complete, the tofu will have begun to crisp and brown around the edges and the squash should be tender. Serve hot.

Puff Pastry

Prep Time: 20 minutes| Cook Time: 10 minutes | Serves 6

- 1 package (8 ounces) cream cheese, softened
- ¼ cup sugar
- 2 tablespoons all-purpose flour
- ½ teaspoon vanilla extract
- 2 large egg yolks
- 1 tablespoon water
- 1 package frozen puff pastry, thawed
- ⅔ cup seedless raspberry jam

1. Mix the cream cheese, sugar, flour, and vanilla extract until smooth, then add 1 egg yolk.
2. Combine the remaining egg yolk with the water. Unfold each sheet of puff pastry on a lightly floured board and roll into a 12-inch square. Cut into nine 4-inch squares.
3. Put 1 tablespoon cream cheese mixture and 1 rounded teaspoon jam on each. Bring 2 opposite corners of pastry over filling, sealing with yolk mixture.
4. Brush the remaining yolk mixture over the tops.
5. Press "Zone 1" and "Zone 2" and then rotate the knob for each zone to select "Air Fry".
6. Set the temperature to 325 degrees F/ 160 degrees C for both zones, and then set the time for 5 minutes to preheat.
7. After preheating, spray the Air-Fryer basket of each zone with cooking spray, line them with parchment paper, and place the pastry on them.
8. Slide the basket into Air Fryer and set the time for 10 minutes.
9. After cooking time is completed, transfer them onto serving plates and serve.

Cinnamon Rolls

Prep Time: 25 minutes| Cook Time: 12 minutes| Serves 6

- 1¾ cups warm water
- 1½ cups sugar divided
- ¼ cup oil
- 2 tablespoons yeast
- ½ tablespoon salt
- 2 eggs
- 5 cups flour
- ½ cup butter, softened
- 1 tablespoons cinnamon
- ½ cup butter, softened
- 2 teaspoons vanilla
- 4 cups powdered sugar
- Milk, for desired consistency

1. In the bowl, combine the water, ½ cup sugar, oil, and yeast; set aside for 15 minutes to allow the yeast to bloom.
2. Combine the salt, eggs, and flour in a mixing bowl. Using the dough hook, mix for 10 minutes. The dough will be slightly damp. Allow 10 minutes for rest.
3. Roll out the dough into a ¼ thick rectangle on a floured work surface. Spread softened butter around the dough's edges.
4. In a bowl, combine the remaining cup of sugar and the cinnamon.
5. Roll into a tube and cut into 12 pieces lengthwise.
6. Combine the softened butter, vanilla, and confectioner's sugar in a mixing bowl to make the frosting.
7. Press "Zone 1" and "Zone 2" and then rotate the knob for each zone to select "Air Fryer".
8. Set the temperature to 360 degrees F/ 180 degrees C for both zones, and then set the time for 5 minutes to preheat.
9. After preheating, arrange cinnamon rolls into the basket of each zone.
10. Slide the baskets into Air Fryer and set the time for 6 minutes.
11. After cooking time is completed, transfer the rolls onto serving plates, top with frosting and serve hot.

Bacon Crescent Rolls

Prep Time: 10 minutes|Cook Time: 10 minutes |Serves 8

- 8 ounces refrigerated crescent rolls
- 6 bacon strips, cooked and crumbled
- 1 teaspoon paprika powder
- Cooking spray

1. Separate the crescent dough into 8 triangles after unrolling it. Set aside 1 tablespoon of bacon.
2. Over the triangles, sprinkle paprika powder and the remaining bacon. Roll it up and spread the leftover bacon on top, lightly pushing it in place.
3. Press "Zone 1" and "Zone 2" and then rotate the knob for each zone to select "Air Fryer".
4. Set the temperature to 300 degrees F/ 150 degrees C for both zones, and then set the time for 5 minutes to preheat.
5. After preheating, spray the Air Fryer basket of each zone with cooking spray. Arrange rolls in a single layer, point side down.
6. Slide the baskets into Air Fryer and set the time for 8 minutes.
7. After cooking time is completed, transfer them onto serving plates and serve hot.

Spanakopita Rolls with Mediterranean Vegetable Salad

Prep time: 15 minutes |Cook time: 15 minutes |Serves 4

- FOR THE SPANAKOPITA ROLLS
- 1 (10-ounce) package chopped frozen spinach, thawed
- 4 ounces feta cheese, crumbled
- 2 large eggs
- 1 teaspoon dried oregano
- ½ teaspoon freshly ground black pepper
- 12 sheets phyllo dough, thawed
- Nonstick cooking spray
- FOR THE ROASTED VEGETABLES
- 1 medium eggplant, diced
- 1 small red onion, cut into 8 wedges
- 1 red bell pepper, sliced
- 2 tablespoons olive oil
- FOR THE SALAD
- 1 (15-ounce) can chickpeas, drained and rinsed
- ¼ cup chopped fresh parsley
- ¼ cup olive oil
- ¼ cup red wine vinegar
- 2 garlic cloves, minced
- ½ teaspoon dried oregano
- ¼ teaspoon kosher salt
- ¼ teaspoon freshly ground black pepper

TO PREP THE SPANAKOPITA ROLLS:

1. Squeeze as much liquid from the spinach as you can and place the spinach in a large bowl. Add the feta, eggs, oregano, and black pepper. Mix well.
2. Lay one sheet of phyllo on a clean work surface and mist it with cooking spray. Place another sheet of phyllo directly on top of the first sheet and mist it with cooking spray. Repeat with a third sheet.
3. Spoon one-quarter of the spinach mixture along one short side of the phyllo. Fold the long sides in over the spinach, then roll up it like a burrito.
4. Repeat this process with the remaining phyllo sheets and spinach mixture to form 4 rolls.

To prep the vegetables: In a large bowl, combine the eggplant, onion, bell pepper, and oil. Mix well.

TO COOK THE ROLLS AND VEGETABLES:

1. seam-si Install a crisper plate in each of the two baskets. Place the spanakopita rolls de down in the Zone 1 basket, and spritz the rolls with cooking spray. Place the vegetables in the Zone 2 basket and insert both baskets in the unit.
2. Select Zone 1, select AIR FRY, set the temperature to 375°F, and set the timer to 10 minutes.
3. Select Zone 2, select ROAST, set the temperature to 375°F, and set the timer to 15 minutes. Select SMART FINISH.
4. Press START/PAUSE to begin cooking.
5. When the Zone 1 timer reads 3 minutes, press START/PAUSE. Remove the basket and use silicone-tipped tongs or a spatula to flip the spanakopita rolls. Reinsert the basket and press START/PAUSE to resume cooking.

6. When cooking is complete, the rolls should be crisp and golden brown and the vegetables tender.

TO ASSEMBLE THE SALAD:

1. Transfer the roasted vegetables to a large bowl. Stir in the chickpeas and parsley.
2. In a small bowl, whisk together the oil, vinegar, garlic, oregano, salt, and black pepper. Pour the dressing over the vegetables and toss to coat. Serve warm.

Berry French Toast Cups

Prep Time: 20 minutes |Cook Time: 20 minutes |Serves 2

- 2 slices bread, cut into small cubes
- ½ cup raspberries
- 2 ounces cream cheese, cut into cubes
- 2 large eggs
- ½ cup 2% milk
- 1 tablespoon maple syrup
- Raspberry syrup:
- 2 teaspoons cornstarch
- ⅓ cup water
- 2 cups fresh or frozen raspberries, divided
- 1 tablespoon lemon juice
- 1 tablespoon maple syrup
- ½ teaspoon grated lemon zest

1. Divide the bread cubes between two buttered 8-ounce custard cups. Sprinkle with raspberries and cream cheese.
2. Finish with the leftover bread. Whisk together the eggs, milk, and syrup in a small bowl; pour over the bread. Refrigerate for at least 1 hour after covering.
3. Press "Zone 1" and "Zone 2" and then rotate the knob for each zone to select "Air Fryer".
4. Set the temperature to 325 degrees F/ 160 degrees C for both zones, and then set the time for 5 minutes to preheat.
5. After preheating, spray the Air Fryer basket of each zone with cooking spray and line them with parchment paper, then place custard cups.
6. Slide them into Air Fryer and set the time for 14 minutes.
7. Meanwhile, whisk together cornstarch and water in a small saucepan until smooth. Add 1-½ cups raspberries, lemon juice, syrup, and lemon zest.
8. Bring to a boil; lower heat. Cook and stir for 2 minutes, or until the sauce has thickened. Strain out the seeds and set them aside to cool.
9. Gently whisk the remaining ½ cup of berries into the syrup in a small bowl.
10. After cooking time is completed, transfer them onto serving plates and serve with maple syrup.

Satay-Style Tempeh with Corn Fritters

Prep time: 15 minutes, plus 15 minutes to marinate|Cook time: 15 minutes|Serves 4

FOR THE TEMPEH

- 1 (8-ounce) package tempeh
- 3 tablespoons fresh lemon juice, divided
- 2 tablespoons soy sauce, divided
- 2 garlic cloves, chopped
- ½ teaspoon ground turmeric
- 2 tablespoons vegetable oil
- ¾ cup canned full-fat coconut milk
- 4 tablespoons peanut butter
- 1 teaspoon light brown sugar
- ½ teaspoon red pepper flakes
- 1 scallion, chopped
- FOR THE CORN FRITTERS
- 2 cups frozen corn, thawed and drained
- 2 scallions, thinly sliced
- ¼ cup chopped fresh cilantro
- ¼ teaspoon kosher salt
- 2 large eggs
- ½ cup all-purpose flour
- 2 tablespoons vegetable oil

TO PREP THE TEMPEH:

1. Slice the tempeh into ¼-inch-thick slabs.
2. In a large bowl, combine 2 tablespoons of lemon juice, 1 tablespoon of soy sauce, the garlic, turmeric, and oil.
3. Add the tempeh to the marinade and toss to coat the pieces. Let marinate for 15 minutes.
4. In a medium bowl, whisk together the coconut milk, peanut butter, remaining 1 tablespoon of lemon juice, remaining 1 tablespoon of soy sauce, brown sugar, red pepper flakes, and scallion. Set aside.

To prep the corn fritters: In a large bowl, combine the corn, scallions, cilantro, and salt. Mix in the eggs and flour until everything is well combined.

TO COOK THE TEMPEH AND FRITTERS:

1. Install a broil rack in the Zone 1 basket. Arrange the tempeh in a single layer on the rack and insert the basket in the unit. Install a crisper plate in the Zone 2 basket. Spoon 2 tablespoons of corn fritter batter into each corner of the basket and drizzle with oil. Flatten slightly with the back of the spoon and insert the basket in the unit.
2. Select Zone 1, select AIR BROIL, set the temperature to 400°F, and set the timer to 8 minutes.
3. Select Zone 2, select AIR FRY, set the temperature to 375°F, and set the timer to 15 minutes. Select SMART FINISH.
4. Press START/PAUSE to begin cooking.
5. When the Zone 2 timer reads 5 minutes, press START/PAUSE. Remove the basket and use silicone-tipped tongs or a spatula to flip the corn fritters. Reinsert the basket and press START/PAUSE to resume cooking.
6. When cooking is complete, the tempeh will be golden brown and the corn fritters set in the center and browned on the edges.
7. Serve the tempeh with the peanut sauce for dipping and the corn fritters on the side.

Bacon Omelet

Prep Time: 15 minutes|Cook Time: 10 minutes|Serves 4

- 8 eggs
- 2 bacon slices, chopped
- 4 sausages, chopped
- 2 yellow onions, chopped

1. In a bowl, crack the eggs and beat well.
2. Add the remaining ingredients and gently stir to combine.
3. Divide the mixture into 2 small baking pans.
4. Press "Zone 1" and "Zone 2" and then rotate the knob for each zone to select "Air Fry".
5. Set the temperature to 320 degrees F/ 160 degrees C for both zones and then set the time for 5 minutes to preheat.
6. After preheating, arrange 1 pan into the basket of each zone.
7. Slide each basket into Air Fryer and set the time for 10 minutes.
8. After cooking time is completed, remove the both pans from Air Fryer.
9. Cut each omelet in wedges and serve hot.

Chapter 4
Poultry Recipes

Turkey Burgers

Prep time: 5 minutes | Cook Time: 13 Minutes | Serves 4

- 1 pound ground turkey
- ¼ cup diced red onion
- 1 tablespoon grilled chicken seasoning
- ½ teaspoon dried parsley
- ½ teaspoon salt
- 4 slices provolone cheese
- 4 whole-grain sandwich buns
- Suggested toppings: lettuce, sliced tomatoes, dill pickles, and mustard

1. Combine the turkey, onion, chicken seasoning, parsley, and salt and mix well.
2. Shape into 4 patties.
3. Cook at 360°F for 11 minutes or until turkey is well done and juices run clear.
4. Top each burger with a slice of cheese and cook 2 minutes to melt.
5. Serve on buns with your favorite toppings.

Turkey Tenderloin With A Lemon Touch

Prep time: 5 minutes | Cook Time: 45 Minutes | Serves 4

- 1 lb boneless, skinless turkey breast tenderloin
- Salt and pepper to taste
- ½ tsp garlic powder
- ½ tsp chili powder
- ½ tsp dried thyme
- 1 lemon, juiced
- 1 tbsp chopped cilantro

1. Preheat air fryer to 350°F.
2. Dry the turkey completely with a paper towel, then season with salt, pepper, garlic powder, chili powder, and thyme.
3. Place the turkey in the frying basket. Squeeze the lemon juice over the turkey and bake for 10 minutes.
4. Turn the turkey and bake for another 10 to 15 minutes.
5. Allow to rest for 10 minutes before slicing. Serve sprinkled with cilantro and enjoy.

Mediterranean Stuffed Chicken Breasts

Prep time: 5 minutes | Cook Time: 24 Minutes | Serves 4

- 4 boneless, skinless chicken breasts
- ½ teaspoon salt
- ½ teaspoon black pepper
- ½ teaspoon garlic powder
- ½ teaspoon paprika
- ½ cup canned artichoke hearts, chopped
- 4 ounces cream cheese
- ¼ cup grated Parmesan cheese

1. Pat the chicken breasts with a paper towel. Using a sharp knife, cut a pouch in the side of each chicken breast for filling.
2. In a small bowl, mix the salt, pepper, garlic powder, and paprika. Season the chicken breasts with this mixture.
3. In a medium bowl, mix together the artichokes, cream cheese, and grated Parmesan cheese. Divide the filling between the 4 breasts, stuffing it inside the pouches. Use toothpicks to close the pouches and secure the filling.
4. Preheat the air fryer to 360°F.
5. Spray the air fryer basket liberally with cooking spray, add the stuffed chicken breasts to the basket, and spray liberally with cooking spray again. Cook for 14 minutes, carefully turn over the chicken breasts, and cook another 10 minutes. Check the temperature at 20 minutes cooking. Chicken breasts are fully cooked when the center measures 165°F. Cook in batches, if needed.

Chicken Cutlets With Broccoli Rabe And Roasted Peppers

Prep time: 5 minutes | Cook Time: 10 Minutes | Serves 2

- ½ bunch broccoli rabe
- olive oil, in a spray bottle
- salt and freshly ground black pepper
- ⅔ cup roasted red pepper strips
- 2 (4-ounce) boneless, skinless chicken breasts
- 2 tablespoons all-purpose flour*
- 1 egg, beaten
- ⅓ cup seasoned breadcrumbs*
- 2 slices aged provolone cheese

1. Bring a medium saucepot of salted water to a boil on the stovetop. Blanch the broccoli rabe for 3 minutes in the boiling water and then drain. When it has cooled a little, squeeze out as much water as possible, drizzle a little olive oil on top, season with salt and black pepper and set aside. Dry the roasted red peppers with a clean kitchen towel and set them aside as well.
2. Place each chicken breast between 2 pieces of plastic wrap. Use a meat pounder to flatten the chicken breasts to about ½-inch thick. Season the chicken on both sides with salt and pepper.
3. Preheat the air fryer to 400°F.
4. Set up a dredging station with three shallow dishes. Place the flour in one dish, the egg in a second dish and the breadcrumbs in a third dish. Coat the chicken on all sides with the flour. Shake off any excess flour and dip the chicken into the egg. Let the excess egg drip off and coat both sides of the chicken in the breadcrumbs. Spray the chicken with olive oil on both sides and transfer to the air fryer basket.
5. Air-fry the chicken at 400°F for 5 minutes. Turn the chicken over and air-fry for another minute. Then, top the chicken breast with the broccoli rabe and roasted peppers. Place a slice of the provolone cheese on top and secure it with a toothpick or two.
6. Air-fry at 360° for 3 to 4 minutes to melt the cheese and warm everything together.

Greek Gyros With Chicken & Rice

Prep time: 5 minutes | Cook Time: 25 Minutes | Serves 4

- 1 lb chicken breasts, cubed
- ¼ cup cream cheese
- 2 tbsp olive oil
- 1 tsp dried oregano
- 1 tsp ground cumin
- 1 tsp ground cinnamon
- ¼ tsp ground nutmeg
- Salt and pepper to taste
- ¼ tsp ground turmeric
- 2 cups cooked rice
- 1 cup Tzatziki sauce

1. Preheat air fryer to 380°F.
2. Put all ingredients in a bowl and mix together until the chicken is coated well.
3. Spread the chicken mixture in the frying basket, then Bake for 10 minutes.
4. Stir the chicken mixture and Bake for an additional 5 minutes.
5. Serve with rice and tzatziki sauce.

Quick Chicken For Filling

Prep time: 5 minutes | Cook Time: 8 Minutes | Serves 2

- 1 pound chicken tenders, skinless and boneless
- ½ teaspoon ground cumin
- ½ teaspoon garlic powder
- cooking spray

1. Sprinkle raw chicken tenders with seasonings.
2. Spray air fryer basket lightly with cooking spray to prevent sticking.
3. Place chicken in air fryer basket in single layer.
4. Cook at 390°F for 4minutes, turn chicken strips over, and cook for an additional 4minutes.
5. Test for doneness. Thick tenders may require an additional minute or two.

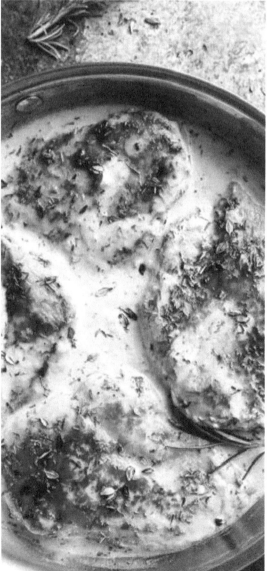

Prosciutto Chicken Rolls

Prep time: 5 minutes | Cook Time: 30 Minutes | Serves 4

- ½ cup chopped broccoli
- ½ cup grated cheddar
- 2 scallions, sliced
- 2 garlic cloves, minced
- 4 prosciutto thin slices
- ¼ cup cream cheese
- Salt and pepper to taste
- ½ tsp dried oregano
- ½ tsp dried basil
- 4 chicken breasts
- 2 tbsp chopped cilantro

1. Preheat air fryer to 375°F. Combine broccoli, scallion, garlic, Cheddar, cream cheese, salt, pepper, oregano, and basil in a small bowl.
2. Prepare the chicken by placing it between two pieces of plastic wrap. Pound the chicken with a meat mallet or heavy can until it is evenly ½-inch thickness.
3. Top each with a slice of prosciutto and spoon ¼ of the cheese mixture in the center of the chicken breast. Fold each breast over the filling and transfer to a greased baking dish. Place the dish in the frying basket and bake for 8 minutes.
4. Flip the chicken and bake for another 8-12 minutes.
5. Allow resting for 5 minutes. Serve warm sprinkled with cilantro and enjoy!

Chicken Chimichangas

Prep time: 15 minutes | Cook Time: 10 Minutes| Serves 4

- 2 cups cooked chicken, shredded
- 2 tablespoons chopped green chiles
- ½ teaspoon oregano
- ½ teaspoon cumin
- ½ teaspoon onion powder
- ¼ teaspoon garlic powder
- salt and pepper
- 8 flour tortillas (6- or 7-inch diameter)
- oil for misting or cooking spray
- Chimichanga Sauce
- 2 tablespoons butter
- 2 tablespoons flour
- 1 cup chicken broth
- ¼ cup light sour cream
- ¼ teaspoon salt
- 2 ounces Pepper Jack or Monterey Jack cheese, shredded

1. Make the sauce by melting butter in a saucepan over medium-low heat. Stir in flour until smooth and slightly bubbly. Gradually add broth, stirring constantly until smooth. Cook and stir 1 minute, until the mixture slightly thickens. Remove from heat and stir in sour cream and salt. Set aside.
2. In a medium bowl, mix together the chicken, chiles, oregano, cumin, onion powder, garlic, salt, and pepper. Stir in 3 to 4 tablespoons of the sauce, using just enough to make the filling moist but not soupy.
3. Divide filling among the 8 tortillas. Place filling down the center of tortilla, stopping about 1 inch from edges. Fold one side of tortilla over filling, fold the two sides in, and then roll up. Mist all sides with oil or cooking spray.
4. Place chimichangas in air fryer basket seam side down. To fit more into the basket, you can stand them on their sides with the seams against the sides of the basket.
5. Cook at 360°F for 10 minutes or until heated through and crispy brown outside.
6. Add the shredded cheese to the remaining sauce. Stir over low heat, warming just until the cheese melts. Don't boil or sour cream may curdle.
7. Drizzle the sauce over the chimichangas.

Parmesan Chicken Meatloaf

Prep time: 15 minutes | Cook Time: 45 Minutes | Serves 4

- 1 ½ tsp evaporated cane sugar
- 1 lb ground chicken
- 4 garlic cloves, minced
- 2 tbsp grated Parmesan
- ¼ cup heavy cream
- ¼ cup minced onion
- 2 tbsp chopped basil
- 2 tbsp chopped parsley
- Salt and pepper to taste
- ½ tsp onion powder
- ½ cup bread crumbs
- ¼ tsp red pepper flakes
- 1 egg
- 1 cup tomato sauce
- ½ tsp garlic powder
- ½ tsp dried thyme
- ½ tsp dried oregano
- 1 tbsp coconut aminos

1. Preheat air fryer to 400°F.
2. Combine chicken, garlic, minced onion, oregano, thyme, basil, salt, pepper, onion powder, Parmesan cheese, red pepper flakes, bread crumbs, egg, and cream in a large bowl.
3. Transfer the chicken mixture to a prepared baking dish.
4. Stir together tomato sauce, garlic powder, coconut aminos, and sugar in a small bowl.
5. Spread over the meatloaf.
6. Loosely cover with foil. Place the pan in the frying basket and bake for 15 minutes.
7. Take the foil off and bake for another 15 minutes.
8. Allow resting for 10 minutes before slicing. Serve sprinkled with parsley.

Hazelnut Chicken Salad With Strawberries

Prep time: 5 minutes | Cook Time: 30 Minutes | Serves 4

- 2 chicken breasts, cubed
- Salt and pepper to taste
- ¾ cup mayonnaise
- 1 tbsp lime juice
- ½ cup chopped hazelnuts
- ½ cup chopped celery
- ½ cup diced strawberries

1. Preheat air fryer to 350°F.
2. Sprinkle chicken cubes with salt and pepper.
3. Place them in the frying basket and Air Fry for 9 minutes, shaking once.
4. Remove to a bowl and leave it to cool.
5. Add the mayonnaise, lime juice, hazelnuts, celery, and strawberries. Serve.

Chicken Pigs In Blankets

Prep time: 5 minutes | Cook Time: 40 Minutes | Serves 4

- 2 tbsp light brown sugar
- 2 tbsp ketchup
- 1 tbsp grainy mustard
- 8 smoked bacon slices
- 1 tsp chopped fresh sage

1. Preheat the air fryer to 350°F. Mix brown sugar, sage, ketchup, and mustard in a bowl and brush the chicken with it.
2. Wrap slices of bacon around the drumsticks and brush with the remaining mix.
3. Line the frying basket with round parchment paper with holes.
4. Set 4 drumsticks on the paper, add a raised rack and set the other drumsticks on it.
5. Bake for 25-35 minutes, moving the bottom drumsticks to the top, top to the bottom, and flipping at about 14-16 minutes.
6. Sprinkle with sage and serve.

Simple Salsa Chicken Thighs

Prep time: 5 minutes | Cook Time: 35 Minutes | Serves 2

- 1 lb boneless, skinless chicken thighs
- 1 cup mild chunky salsa
- ½ tsp taco seasoning
- 2 lime wedges for serving

1. Preheat air fryer to 350°F. Add chicken thighs into a baking pan and pour salsa and taco seasoning over.
2. Place the pan in the frying basket and Air Fry for 30 minutes until golden brown.
3. Serve with lime wedges.

Asian-style Orange Chicken

Prep time: 5 minutes | Cook Time: 25 Minutes | Serves 4

- 1 lb chicken breasts, cubed
- Salt and pepper to taste
- 6 tbsp cornstarch
- 1 cup orange juice
- ¼ cup orange marmalade
- ¼ cup ketchup
- ½ tsp ground ginger
- 2 tbsp soy sauce
- 1 1/3 cups edamame beans

1. Preheat the air fryer to 375°F. Sprinkle the cubes with salt and pepper.
2. Coat with 4 tbsp of cornstarch and set aside on a wire rack.
3. Mix the orange juice, marmalade, ketchup, ginger, soy sauce, and the remaining cornstarch in a cake pan, then stir in the beans.
4. Set the pan in the frying basket and Bake for 5-8 minutes, stirring once during cooking until the sauce is thick and bubbling.
5. Remove from the fryer and set aside.
6. Put the chicken in the frying basket and fry for 10-12 minutes, shaking the basket once.
7. Stir the chicken into the sauce and beans in the pan.
8. Return to the fryer and reheat for 2 minutes.

Chicken Stuffed Mushrooms

Prep Time: 15 minutes| Cook Time: 15 minutes| Serves 6

- 6 large fresh mushrooms, stems removed
- Stuffing:
- ½ cup chicken meat, cubed
- 1 (4 ounces) package cream cheese, softened
- ¼ lb. imitation crabmeat, flaked
- 1 cup butter
- 1 garlic clove, peeled and minced
- Black pepper and salt to taste
- Garlic powder to taste
- Crushed red pepper to taste

1. Melt and heat butter in a skillet over medium heat.
2. Add chicken and sauté for 5 minutes.
3. Add in all the remaining ingredients for the stuffing.
4. Cook for 5 minutes, then turn off the heat.
5. Allow the mixture to cool. Stuff each mushroom with a tablespoon of this mixture.
6. Divide the stuffed mushrooms in the two crisper plates.
7. Return the crisper plate to the Ninja Foodi Dual Zone Air Fryer.
8. Choose the Air Fry mode for Zone 1 and set the temperature to 375 degrees F/ 190 degrees C and the time to 15 minutes.
9. Select the "MATCH" button to copy the settings for Zone 2.
10. Initiate cooking by pressing the START/STOP button. 11. Serve warm.

Chapter 5
Meat Recipes

Beef & Broccoli

Prep Time: 12 Minutes | Cook Time: 12 Minutes | Serves 4

- 12 ounces Teriyaki sauce, divided
- ½ tablespoon garlic powder
- ¼ cup soy sauce
- 1 pound raw sirloin steak, thinly sliced
- 2 cups broccoli, cut into florets
- 2 teaspoons olive oil
- Salt and black pepper, to taste

1. Mix the Teriyaki sauce, salt, garlic powder, black pepper, soy sauce, and olive oil in a zip-lock bag.
2. Add the beef and let it marinate for 2 hours.
3. Drain the beef from the marinade.
4. Toss the broccoli with oil, teriyaki sauce, and salt and black pepper and place in the zone 1 basket.
5. Place the beef in both baskets and set it to SYNC button.
6. Hit START/STOP button and let the cooking cycle complete.
7. Once it's done, take out the beef and broccoli and serve with the leftover Teriyaki sauce and cooked rice.

Beef Ribs

Prep Time: 10 Minutes | Cook Time: 15 Minutes | Serves 2

- 4 tablespoons BBQ spice rub
- 1 tablespoon kosher salt and black pepper
- 3 tablespoons brown sugar
- 2 pounds of beef ribs cut in thirds
- 1 cup BBQ sauce
- Oil spray

1. In a small bowl, add salt, pepper, brown sugar, and BBQ spice rub.
2. Grease the ribs with oil spray from both sides and then rub it with BBQ the spice.
3. Divide the ribs into both baskets and set zone 1to AIR FRY mode at 375 degrees F for 15 minutes.
4. Press MATCH for zone 2.
5. Hit START/STOP button and let the air fryer cook the ribs.
6. Once done, serve with a coating BBQ sauce.

Chinese BBQ Pork

Prep Time: 15 Minutes | Cook Time: 25-35 Minutes | Serves 2

- 4 tablespoons soy sauce
- ¼ cup red wine
- 2 tablespoons oyster sauce
- ¼ tablespoon hoisin sauce
- ¼ cup honey
- ¼ cup brown sugar
- Pinch of salt
- Pinch of black pepper
- 1 teaspoon ginger garlic, paste
- 1 teaspoon five-spice powder
- 1.5 pounds pork shoulder, sliced

1. Take a bowl and mix all the sauce Ingredients: well.
2. Transfer half of it to a sauce pan and cook for 10 minutes, and then set it aside.
3. Let the pork marinate in the remaining sauce for 2 hours.
4. Place the pork slices in the air fryer basket in zone 1 and set it to AIR FRY mode at 450 degrees F for 25 minutes.
5. Make sure the internal temperature is above 160 degrees F once cooked.
6. If not, add a few more minutes to the overall cooking time.
7. Once done, take it out and baste it with the cooked sauce.
8. Serve and Enjoy.

Ham Burger Patties

Prep Time: 15 Minutes | Cook Time: 17 Minutes | Serves 2

- 1 pound ground beef
- Salt and pepper, to taste
- ½ teaspoon red chili powder
- ¼ teaspoon coriander powder
- 2 tablespoons chopped onion
- 1 green chili, chopped
- Oil spray for greasing
- 2 large potato wedges

1. Grease the air fryer baskets with oil.
2. Place the potato wedges into the zone 1 basket.
3. Add the minced beef, salt, pepper, chili powder, coriander powder, green chili, and chopped onion to a bowl and mix well.
4. With wet hands, make two burger patties out of the mixture and place in zone 2 of the air fryer.
5. Set the time for zone 1 to 12 minutes on AIR FRY mode at 400 degrees F.
6. Select the MATCH button for zone 2.
7. Once the time is up, take the baskets out and flip the patties and shake the potato wedges.
8. Set zone 1 for 4 minutes at 400 degrees F on AIR FRY.
9. Select the MATCH button for the second basket.
10. Once it's done, serve and enjoy.

Glazed Steak Recipe

Prep Time: 15 Minutes | Cook Time: 25 Minutes | Serves 2

- 1 pound beef steaks
- ½ cup, soy sauce
- Salt and black pepper, to taste
- 1 tablespoon vegetable oil
- 1 teaspoon grated ginger
- 4 cloves garlic, minced
- ¼ cup brown sugar

1. Whisk together soy sauce, salt, pepper, vegetable oil, garlic, brown sugar, and ginger in a bowl.
2. Once a paste is made from the mixture, rub the steak with it and let it sit for 30 minutes.
3. Add the steak to the air fryer basket and set it to MAX CRISP mode at 400 degrees F for 18-22 minutes.
4. After 10 minutes, hit START/STOP and take it out to flip and return to the air fryer.
5. Once the time is complete, take out the steak and let it rest. Serve by cutting into slices.
6. Enjoy.

Short Ribs & Root Vegetables

Prep Time: 15 Minutes | Cook Time: 45 Minutes | Serves 2

- 1 pound beef short ribs, bone-in and trimmed
- Salt and black pepper, to taste
- 2 tablespoons canola oil, divided
- ¼ cup red wine
- 3 tablespoons brown sugar
- 2 cloves garlic, peeled, minced
- 4 carrots, peeled, cut into 1-inch pieces
- 2 parsnips, peeled, cut into 1-inch pieces
- ½ cup pearl onions

1. Season the ribs with salt and black pepper and rub a small amount of canola oil on both sides.
2. Place the ribs in zone 1 basket of the air fryer.
3. Next, take a bowl and add the pearl onions, parsnips, carrots, garlic, brown sugar, red wine, salt, and black pepper.
4. Add the vegetable mixture to the zone 2 basket.
5. Press the Sync button.
6. Hit START/STOP button so the cooking cycle begins.
7. Once the cooking is complete, take out and serve.
8. Enjoy it hot.

Yogurt Lamb Chops

Prep Time: 10 Minutes | Cook Time: 20 Minutes | Serves 2

- 1½ cups plain Greek yogurt
- 1 lemon, juice only
- 1 teaspoon ground cumin
- 1 teaspoon ground coriander
- ¾ teaspoon ground turmeric
- ¼ teaspoon ground allspice
- 10 rib lamb chops (1–1¼ inches thick cut)

1. In a bowl, add all the Ingredients: and rub the chops well. Let it marinate for an hour in the refrigerator.
2. After an hour take out the chops and layer the air fryer baskets with parchment paper.
3. Divide the chops between both the baskets.
4. Set the time for zone 1 to 20 minutes at 400 degrees F on AIR FRY.
5. Select the MATCH button for the zone 2 basket.
6. Hit START/STOP button and then wait for the chops to cook.
7. Once done, serve and enjoy.

Steak Fajitas With Onions and Peppers

Prep Time: 10 minutes | Cook Time: 15 minutes | Serves 6

- 1 pound steak
- 1 green bell pepper, sliced
- 1 yellow bell pepper, sliced
- 1 red bell pepper, sliced
- ½ cup sliced white onions
- 1 packet gluten-free fajita seasoning
- Olive oil spray

1. Thinly slice the steak against the grain. These should be about ¼-inch slices.
2. Mix the steak with the peppers and onions.
3. Evenly coat with the fajita seasoning.
4. Install a crisper plate in both drawers. Place half the steak mixture in the zone 1 drawer and half in zone 2's, then insert the drawers into the unit.
5. Select zone 1, select AIR FRY, set temperature to 390°F, and set time to 15 minutes. Select MATCH to match zone 2 settings to zone 1. Press the START/STOP button to begin cooking.
6. When the time reaches 10 minutes, press START/STOP to pause the unit. Remove the drawers and flip the steak strips. Re-insert the drawers into the unit and press START/STOP to resume cooking.

Jerk-Rubbed Pork Loin With Carrots and Sage

Prep Time: 10 minutes | Cook Time: 35 minutes | Serves 4

- 1½ pounds pork loin
- 3 teaspoons canola oil, divided
- 2 tablespoons jerk seasoning
- 1-pound carrots, peeled, cut into 1-inch pieces
- 1 tablespoon honey
- ½ teaspoon kosher salt
- ½ teaspoon chopped fresh sage

1. Place the pork loin in a pan or a dish with a high wall. Using a paper towel, pat the meat dry.
2. Rub 2 teaspoons of canola oil evenly over the pork with your hands. Then spread the jerk seasoning evenly over it with your hands.
3. Allow the pork loin to marinate for at least 10 minutes or up to 8 hours in the refrigerator after wrapping it in plastic wrap or sealing it in a plastic bag.
4. Toss the carrots with the remaining canola oil and ½ teaspoon of salt in a medium mixing bowl.
5. Place a crisper plate in each of the drawers. Put the marinated pork loin in the zone 1 drawer and place it in the unit. Place the carrots in the zone 2 drawer and place the drawer in the unit.
6. Select zone 1 and select AIR FRY. Set the temperature to 390°F and the time setting to 25 minutes. Select zone 2 and select AIR FRY. Set the temperature to 390°F and the time setting to 16 minutes. Select SYNC. Press START/STOP to begin cooking.
7. Check the pork loin for doneness after the zones have finished cooking. When the internal temperature of the loin hits 145°F on an instant-read thermometer, the pork is ready.
8. Allow the pork loin to rest for at least 5 minutes on a plate or cutting board.
9. Combine the carrots and sage in a mixing bowl.
10. When the pork loin has rested, slice it into the desired thickness of slices and serve with the carrots.

Korean BBQ Beef

Prep Time: 15 minutes| Cook Time: 30 minutes| Serves 6

- FOR THE MEAT
- 1 pound flank steak or thinly sliced steak
- ¼ cup corn starch
- Coconut oil spray
- FOR THE SAUCE
- ½ cup soy sauce or gluten-free soy sauce
- ½ cup brown sugar
- 2 tablespoons white wine vinegar
- 1 clove garlic, crushed
- 1 tablespoon hot chili sauce
- 1 teaspoon ground ginger
- ½ teaspoon sesame seeds
- 1 tablespoon corn starch
- 1 tablespoon water

1. To begin, prepare the steak. Thinly slice it in that toss it in the corn starch to be coated thoroughly. Spray the tops with some coconut oil.
2. Spray the crisping plates and drawers with the coconut oil.
3. Place the crisping plates into the drawers. Place the steak strips into each drawer. Insert both drawers into the unit.
4. Select zone 1, Select AIR FRY, set the temperature to 375°F, and set time to 30 minutes. Select MATCH to match zone 2 settings with zone 1. Press the START/STOP button to begin cooking.
5. While the steak is cooking, add the sauce Ingredients: EXCEPT for the corn starch and water to a medium saucepan.
6. Warm it up to a low boil, then whisk in the corn starch and water.
7. Carefully remove the steak and pour the sauce over. Mix well.

Spicy Lamb Chops

Prep Time: 15 Minutes | Cook Time: 15 Minutes| Serves 4

- 12 lamb chops, bone-in
- Salt and black pepper, to taste
- ½ teaspoon lemon zest
- 1 tablespoon lemon juice
- 1 teaspoon paprika
- 1 teaspoon garlic powder
- ½ teaspoon Italian seasoning
- ¼ teaspoon onion powder

1. Add the lamb chops to the bowl and sprinkle with salt, garlic powder, Italian seasoning, onion powder, black pepper, lemon zest, lemon juice, and paprika.
2. Rub the chops well, and divide them between both the baskets of the air fryer.
3. Set zone 1 basket to 400 degrees F, for 15 minutes on AIR FRY mode.
4. Select MATCH for zone 2 basket.
5. After 10 minutes, take out the baskets and flip the chops. Cook for the remaining minutes, and then serve.

Garlic Butter Steaks

Prep Time: 120 minutes | Cook Time: 25 minutes | Serves 2

- 2 (6 ounces each) sirloin steaks or ribeyes
- 2 tablespoons unsalted butter
- 1 clove garlic, crushed
- ½ teaspoon dried parsley
- ½ teaspoon dried rosemary
- Salt and pepper, to taste

1. Season the steaks with salt and pepper and set them to rest for about 2 hours before cooking.
2. Put the butter in a bowl. Add the garlic, parsley, and rosemary. Allow the butter to soften.
3. Whip together with a fork or spoon once the butter has softened.
4. When you're ready to cook, install a crisper plate in both drawers. Place the sirloin steaks in a single layer in each drawer. Insert the drawers into the unit.
5. Select zone 1, select AIR FRY, set temperature to 360°F, and set time to 10 minutes. Select MATCH to match zone 2 settings to zone 1. Select START/STOP to begin.
6. Once done, serve with the garlic butter.

Parmesan Pork Chops

Prep Time: 5 minutes | Cook Time: 20 minutes | Serves 4

- 4 boneless pork chops
- 2 tablespoons extra-virgin olive oil
- ½ cup freshly grated parmesan
- 1 teaspoon kosher salt
- 1 teaspoon paprika
- 1 teaspoon garlic powder
- 1 teaspoon onion powder
- ½ teaspoon freshly ground black pepper

1. Dry the pork chops with paper towels before brushing both sides with oil.
2. Combine the parmesan and spices in a medium mixing bowl. Coat the pork chops on both sides with the parmesan mixture.
3. Install a crisper plate in both drawers. Place half the pork chops in the zone 1 drawer and half in zone 2's, then insert the drawers into the unit.
4. Select zone 1, select AIR FRY, set temperature to 390°F, and set time to 20 minutes. Select MATCH to match zone 2 settings to zone 1. Press the START/STOP button to begin cooking.
5. When the time reaches 10 minutes, press START/STOP to pause the unit. Remove the drawers and flip the chicken. Re-insert the drawers into the unit and press START/STOP to resume cooking.

Meatloaf

Prep Time: 10 minutes | Cook Time: 25 minutes | Serves 6

- FOR THE MEATLOAF
- 2 pounds ground beef
- 2 eggs, beaten
- 2 cups old-fashioned oats, regular or gluten-free
- ½ cup evaporated milk
- ½ cup chopped onion
- ½ teaspoon garlic salt
- FOR THE SAUCE
- 1 cup ketchup
- ¾ cup brown sugar, packed
- ¼ cup chopped onion
- ½ teaspoon liquid smoke
- ¼ teaspoon garlic powder
- Olive oil cooking spray

1. In a large bowl, combine all the meatloaf Ingredients:.
2. Spray 2 sheets of foil with olive oil cooking spray.
3. Form the meatloaf mixture into a loaf shape, cut in half, and place each half on one piece of foil.
4. Roll the foil up a bit on the sides. Allow it to be slightly open.
5. Put all the sauce Ingredients: in a saucepan and whisk until combined on medium-low heat. This should only take 1–2 minutes
6. Install a crisper plate in both drawers. Place half the meatloaf in the zone 1 drawer and half in zone 2's, then insert the drawers into the unit.
7. Select zone 1, select AIR FRY, set temperature to 390°F, and set time to 25 minutes. Select MATCH to match zone 2 settings to zone 1. Press the START/STOP button to begin cooking.
8. When the time reaches 20 minutes, press START/STOP to pause the unit. Remove the drawers and coat the meatloaf with the sauce using a brush. Re-insert the drawers into the unit and press START/STOP to resume cooking.
9. Carefully remove and serve.

Pork Chops

Prep Time: 10 Minutes | Cook Time: 17 Minutes | Serves 2

- 1 tablespoon rosemary, chopped
- Salt and black pepper, to taste
- 2 garlic cloves
- 1-inch ginger
- 2 tablespoons olive oil
- 8 pork chops

1. Take a blender and pulse rosemary, salt, pepper, garlic cloves, ginger, and olive oil.
2. Rub this marinade over the pork chops and let it rest for 1 hour.
3. Divide the chops into both the baskets. Set zone 1 to AIR FRY mode for 17 minutes.
4. Select the MATCH button for zone 2.
5. Once done, take out and serve hot.

Breaded Pork Chops

Prep Time: 10 minutes | Cook Time: 10 minutes | Serves 4

- 4 boneless, center-cut pork chops, 1-inch thick
- 1 teaspoon Cajun seasoning
- 1½ cups cheese and garlic-flavored croutons
- 2 eggs
- Cooking spray

1. Season both sides of the pork chops with the Cajun seasoning on a platter.
2. In a small food processor, pulse the croutons until finely chopped; transfer to a shallow plate.
3. In a separate shallow bowl, lightly beat the eggs.
4. Dip the pork chops in the egg, allowing any excess to drip off. Then place the chops in the crouton crumbs. Coat the chops in cooking spray.
5. Install a crisper plate in both drawers. Place half the pork chops in the zone 1 drawer and half in zone 2's, then insert the drawers into the unit.
6. Select zone 1, select ROAST, set temperature to 390°F, and set time to 10 minutes. Select MATCH to match zone 2 settings to zone 1. Press the START/STOP button to begin cooking.
7. When the time reaches 6 minutes, press START/STOP to pause the unit. Remove the drawers and flip the chops. Reinsert the drawers into the unit and press START/STOP to resume cooking.
8. When cooking is complete, serve and enjoy!

Steak in Air Fry

Prep Time: 15 Minutes | Cook Time: 20 Minutes | Serves 1

- 2 teaspoons canola oil
- 1 tablespoon Montreal Steak seasoning
- 1 pound beef steak

1. Season the steak on both sides with canola oil and then rub a generous amount of steak seasoning all over.
2. Put the steak in the air fryer basket in zone 1and set it to MAX CRISP at 450 degrees F for 20-22 minutes.
3. After 7 minutes, hit pause, take out the basket to flip the steak and cover it with foil on top for the remaining 14 minutes.
4. Once done, serve the medium-rare steak after it has rested for 10 minutes.
5. Serve by cutting into slices.
6. Enjoy.

Juicy Pork Chops

Prep Time: 5 minutes | Cook Time: 15 minutes | Serves 4

- 4 thick-cut pork chops
- Salt and pepper, to taste
- 2 tablespoons brown sugar
- 1 teaspoon chili powder
- ½ teaspoon paprika
- 1 teaspoon Italian seasoning
- 1 teaspoon garlic powder

1. Salt and pepper the pork chops.
2. Add the brown sugar, chili powder, paprika, Italian seasoning, and garlic powder to a small bowl. Combine well. Rub the mixture on the pork chops.
3. Install a crisper plate in both drawers. Place half the pork chops in the zone 1 drawer and half in zone 2's. Insert the drawers into the unit.
4. Select zone 1, select AIR FRY, set temperature to 400°F, and set time to 15 minutes. Select MATCH to match zone 2 settings to zone 1. Press the START/STOP button to begin cooking.
5. When the time reaches 11 minutes, press START/STOP to pause the unit. Remove the drawers and flip the chops. Re-insert the drawers into the unit and press START/STOP to resume cooking.
6. Serve and enjoy!

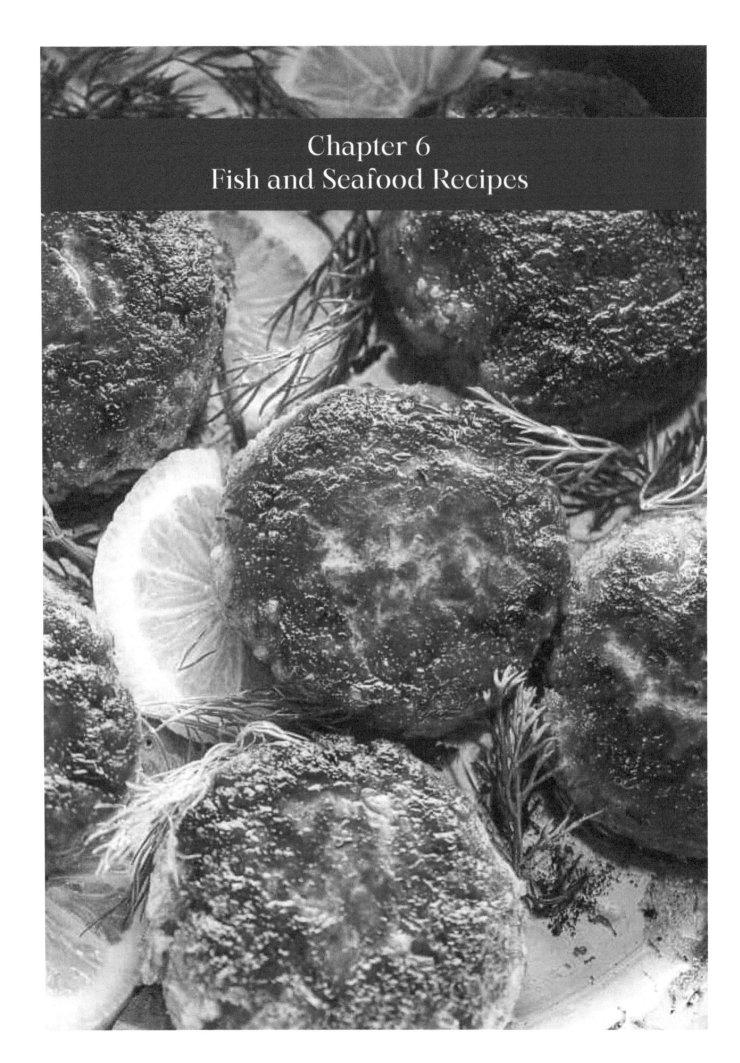

Chapter 6
Fish and Seafood Recipes

Salmon Patties

Prep Time: 15 minutes| Cook Time: 18 minutes| Serves 8

- 1 lb. fresh Atlantic salmon side
- ¼ cup avocado, mashed
- ¼ cup cilantro, diced
- 1 ½ teaspoons yellow curry powder
- ½ teaspoons sea salt
- ¼ cup, 4 teaspoons tapioca starch
- 2 brown eggs
- ½ cup coconut flakes
- Coconut oil, melted, for brushing
- 2 teaspoons organic coconut oil, melted
- 6 cups arugula & spinach mix, tightly packed
- Pinch of sea salt

1. Remove the fish skin and dice the flesh.
2. Place in a large bowl. Add cilantro, avocado, salt, and curry powder mix gently.
3. Add tapioca starch and mix well again.
4. Make 8 salmon patties out of this mixture, about a half-inch thick.
5. Place them on a baking sheet lined with wax paper and freeze them for 20 minutes.
6. Place ¼ cup tapioca starch and coconut flakes on a flat plate.
7. Dip the patties in the whisked egg, then coat the frozen patties in the starch and flakes. 8. Place half of the patties in each of the crisper plate and spray them with cooking oil
8. Return the crisper plate to the Ninja Foodi Dual Zone Air Fryer.
9. Choose the Air Fry mode for Zone 1 and set the temperature to 390 degrees F/ 200 degrees C and the time to 17 minutes.
10. Select the "MATCH" button to copy the settings for Zone 2.
11. Initiate cooking by pressing the START/STOP button.
12. Flip the patties once cooked halfway through, then resume cooking.
13. Sauté arugula with spinach in coconut oil in a pan for 30 seconds.
14. Serve the patties with sautéed greens mixture

Scallops with Greens

Prep Time: 15 minutes| Cook Time: 13 minutes | Serves 8

- ¾ cup heavy whipping cream
- 1 tablespoon tomato paste
- 1 tablespoon chopped fresh basil
- 1 teaspoon garlic, minced
- ½ teaspoons salt
- ½ teaspoons pepper
- 12 ounces frozen spinach thawed
- 8 jumbo sea scallops
- Vegetable oil to spray

1. Season the scallops with vegetable oil, salt, and pepper in a bowl

2. Mix cream with spinach, basil, garlic, salt, pepper, and tomato paste in a bowl.
3. Pour this mixture over the scallops and mix gently.
4. Divide the scallops in the Air Fryers Baskets without using the crisper plate.
5. Return the crisper plate to the Ninja Foodi Dual Zone Air Fryer.
6. Choose the Air Fry mode for Zone 1 and set the temperature to 390 degrees F/ 200 degrees C and the time to 13 minutes.
7. Select the "MATCH" button to copy the settings for Zone 2.
8. Initiate cooking by pressing the START/STOP button.
9. Serve right away

Fish Sandwich

Prep Time: 15 minutes | Cook Time: 22 minutes | Serves 4

- 4 small cod fillets, skinless
- Salt and black pepper, to taste
- 2 tablespoons flour
- ¼ cup dried breadcrumbs
- Spray oil
- 9 ounces of frozen peas
- 1 tablespoon creme fraiche
- 12 capers
- 1 squeeze of lemon juice
- 4 bread rolls, cut in halve

1. First, coat the cod fillets with flour, salt, and black pepper.
2. Then coat the fish with breadcrumbs.
3. Divide the coated codfish in the two crisper plates and spray them with cooking spray. 4. Return the crisper plate to the Ninja Foodi Dual Zone Air Fryer.
4. Choose the Air Fry mode for Zone 1 and set the temperature to 390 degrees F/ 200 degrees C and the time to 17 minutes.
5. Select the "MATCH" button to copy the settings for Zone 2.
6. Initiate cooking by pressing the START/STOP button.
7. Meanwhile, boil peas in hot water for 5 minutes until soft.
8. Then drain the peas and transfer them to the blender.
9. Add capers, lemon juice, and crème fraiche to the blender.
10. Blend until it makes a smooth mixture.
11. Spread the peas crème mixture on top of 2 lower halves of the bread roll, and place the fish fillets on it.
12. Place the remaining bread slices on top.
13. Serve fresh.

Salmon Quiche

Prep Time: 15 minutes| Cook Time: 20 minutes| Serves 4

- 11 ounces salmon fillets, chopped
- Salt and ground black pepper, as required
- 1 tablespoon fresh lemon juice
- 2 egg yolks
- 7 tablespoons chilled butter
- 1⅓ cups flour
- 2 tablespoons cold water
- 4 eggs
- 6 tablespoons whipping cream
- 2 scallions, chopped

1. In a bowl, mix together the salmon, salt, black pepper and lemon juice. Set aside.
2. In another bowl, add egg yolk, butter, flour and water and mix until a dough forms.
3. Divide the dough into 2 portions.
4. Place each dough onto a floured smooth surface and roll into about 7-inch round.
5. Place each rolled dough into a quiche pan and press firmly in the bottom and along the edges.
6. Then trim the excess edges.
7. In a small bowl, add the eggs, cream, salt and black pepper and beat until well combined.
8. Place the cream mixture over each crust evenly and top with the salmon, followed by the scallion.
9. Press "Zone 1" and "Zone 2" of Ninja Foodi 2-Basket Air Fryer and then rotate the knob for each zone to select "Air Fry".
10. Set the temperature to 355 degrees F/ 180 degrees C for both zones and then set the time for 5 minutes to preheat.
11. After preheating, arrange 1 quiche pan into the basket of each zone.
12. Slide each basket into Air Fryer and set the time for 20 minutes.
13. After cooking time is completed, remove the quiche pans from Air Fryer.
14. Cut each quiche in 2 portions and serve hot.

Shrimp with Lemon and Pepper

Prep Time: 5 minutes | Cook Time: 10 minutes | Serves 4

- 1-pound medium raw shrimp, peeled and deveined
- ½ cup olive oil
- 2 tablespoons lemon juice
- 1 teaspoon black pepper
- ½ teaspoon salt

1. Place the shrimp in a Ziploc bag with the olive oil, lemon juice, salt, and pepper. Carefully combine all the ingredients.
2. Install a crisper plate in both drawers. Divide the shrimp equally into the two drawers. Insert the drawers into the unit.
3. Select zone 1, then AIR FRY, then set the temperature to 360 degrees F/ 180 degrees C with a 10-minute timer. To match zone 2 settings to zone 1, choose MATCH. To begin, select START/STOP.
4. Remove the shrimp from the drawers after the timer has finished.

Garlic Butter Salmon

Prep Time: 5 minutes | Cook Time: 10 minutes | Serves 4

- 4 (6-ounce) boneless, skin-on salmon fillets (preferably wild-caught)
- 4 tablespoons butter, melted
- 2 teaspoons garlic, minced
- 2 teaspoons fresh Italian parsley, chopped (or ¼ teaspoon dried)
- Salt and pepper to taste

1. Season the fresh salmon with salt and pepper.
2. Mix together the melted butter, garlic, and parsley in a bowl.
3. Baste the salmon fillets with the garlic butter mixture.
4. Place a crisper plate in each drawer. Put 2 fillets in each drawer. Put the drawers inside the unit.
5. Select zone 1, then AIR FRY, then set the temperature to 360 degrees F/ 180 degrees C with a 10-minute timer. To match zone 2 settings to zone 1, choose MATCH. To begin, select START/STOP.
6. Remove the salmon from the drawers after the timer has finished.

Flavorful Salmon with Green Beans

Prep Time: 5 minutes | Cook Time: 10 minutes | Serves 4

- 4 ounces green beans
- 1 tablespoon canola oil
- 4 (6-ounce) salmon fillets
- 1/3 cup prepared sesame-ginger sauce
- Kosher salt, to taste
- Black pepper, to taste

1. Toss the green beans with a teaspoon each of salt and pepper in a large bowl.
2. Place a crisper plate in each drawer. Place the green beans in the zone 1 drawer and insert it into the unit. Place the salmon into the zone 2 drawer and place it into the unit.
3. Select zone 1, then AIR FRY, and set the temperature to 390 degrees F/ 200 degrees C with a 10-minute timer.
4. Select zone 2, then AIR FRY, and set the temperature to 390 degrees F/ 200 degrees C with a 15-minute timer. Select SYNC. To begin cooking, press the START/STOP button.
5. Press START/STOP to pause the unit when the zone 2 timer reaches 9 minutes. Remove the salmon from the drawer and toss it in the sesame-ginger sauce. To resume cooking, replace the drawer in the device and press START/STOP.
6. When cooking is complete, serve the salmon and green beans immediately.

Bacon-Wrapped Shrimp

Prep Time: 45 minutes | Cook Time: 10 minutes | Serves 8

- 24 jumbo raw shrimp, deveined with tail on, fresh or thawed from frozen
- 8 slices bacon, cut into thirds
- 1 tablespoon olive oil
- 1 teaspoon paprika
- 1–2 cloves minced garlic
- 1 tablespoon finely chopped fresh parsley

1. Combine the olive oil, paprika, garlic, and parsley in a small bowl.
2. If necessary, peel the raw shrimp, leaving the tails on.
3. Add the shrimp to the oil mixture. Toss to coat well.
4. Wrap a piece of bacon around the middle of each shrimp and place seam-side down on a small baking dish.
5. Refrigerate for 30 minutes before cooking.
6. Place a crisper plate in each drawer. Put the shrimp in a single layer in each drawer. Insert the drawers into the unit.
7. Select zone 1, then AIR FRY, then set the temperature to 360 degrees F/ 180 degrees C with a 10-minute timer. To match zone 2 settings to zone 1, choose MATCH. To begin, select START/STOP.
8. Remove the shrimp from the drawers when the cooking time is over.

Honey Sriracha Mahi Mahi

Prep Time: 5 minutes | Cook Time: 7 minutes | Serves 4

- 3 pounds mahi-mahi
- 6 tablespoons honey
- 4 tablespoons sriracha
- Salt, to taste
- Cooking spray

1. In a small bowl, mix the sriracha sauce and honey. Mix well.
2. Season the fish with salt and pour the honey mixture over it. Let it sit at room temperature for 20 minutes.
3. Place a crisper plate in each drawer. Put the fish in a single layer in each. Insert the drawers into the unit.
4. Select zone 1, then AIR FRY, then set the temperature to 400 degrees F/ 200 degrees C with a 7-minute timer. To match zone 2 settings to zone 1, choose MATCH. To begin, select START/STOP.
5. Remove the fish from the drawers after the timer has finished.

Salmon with Fennel Salad

Prep Time: 10 minutes| Cook Time: 17 minutes | Serves 4

- 2 teaspoons fresh parsley, chopped
- 1 teaspoon fresh thyme, chopped
- 1 teaspoon salt
- 4 (6-oz) skinless center-cut salmon fillets
- 2 tablespoons olive oil
- 4 cups fennel, sliced
- ⅔ cup Greek yogurt
- 1 garlic clove, grated
- 2 tablespoons orange juice
- 1 teaspoon lemon juice
- 2 tablespoons fresh dill, chopped

1. Preheat your Ninja Foodi Dual Zone Air Fryer to 200 degrees F/ 95 degrees C.
2. Mix ½ teaspoon of salt, thyme, and parsley in a small bowl.
3. Brush the salmon with oil first, then rub liberally rub the herb mixture.
4. Place 2 salmon fillets in each of the crisper plate.
5. Return the crisper plate to the Ninja Foodi Dual Zone Air Fryer.
6. Choose the Air Fry mode for Zone 1 and set the temperature to 390 degrees F/ 200 degrees C and the time to 17 minutes.
7. Select the "MATCH" button to copy the settings for Zone 2.
8. Initiate cooking by pressing the START/STOP button.
9. Meanwhile, mix fennel with garlic, yogurt, lemon juice, orange juice, remaining salt, and dill in a mixing bowl.
10. Serve the air fried salmon fillets with fennel salad.
11. Enjoy.

Crusted Shrimp

Prep Time: 20 minutes | Cook Time: 13 minutes| Serves 4

- 1 lb. shrimp
- ½ cup flour, all-purpose
- 1 teaspoon salt
- ½ teaspoon baking powder
- ⅔ cup water
- 2 cups coconut shred
- ½ cup bread crumbs

1. In a small bowl, whisk together flour, salt, water, and baking powder. Set aside for 5 minutes.
2. In another shallow bowl, toss bread crumbs with coconut shreds together.
3. Dredge shrimp in liquid, then coat in coconut mixture, making sure it's totally covered. 4. Repeat until all shrimp are coated.
4. Spread half of the shrimp in each crisper plate and spray them with cooking oil.
5. Return the crisper plates to the Ninja Foodi Dual Zone Air Fryer.
6. Choose the Air Fry mode for Zone 1 and set the temperature to 390 degrees F/ 200 degrees C and the time to 13 minutes.
7. Select the "MATCH" button to copy the settings for Zone 2.
8. Initiate cooking by pressing the START/STOP button.
9. Shake the baskets once cooked halfway, then resume cooking.
10. Serve with your favorite dip.

Honey Teriyaki Tilapia

Prep Time: 5 minutes | Cook Time: 10 minutes | Serve 4

- 8 tablespoons low-sodium teriyaki sauce
- 3 tablespoons honey
- 2 garlic cloves, minced
- 2 tablespoons extra virgin olive oil
- 3 pieces tilapia (each cut into 2 pieces)

1. Combine all the first 4 ingredients to make the marinade.
2. Pour the marinade over the tilapia and let it sit for 20 minutes.
3. Place a crisper plate in each drawer. Place the tilapia in the drawers. Insert the drawers into the unit.
4. Select zone 1, then AIR FRY, then set the temperature to 360 degrees F/ 180 degrees C with a 10-minute timer. To match zone 2 settings to zone 1, choose MATCH. To begin, select START/STOP.
5. Remove the tilapia from the drawers after the timer has finished.

Fried Tilapia

Prep Time: 5 minutes | Cook Time: 20 minutes | Serves 4

- 4 fresh tilapia fillets, approximately 6 ounces each
- 2 teaspoons olive oil
- 2 teaspoons chopped fresh chives
- 2 teaspoons chopped fresh parsley
- 1 teaspoon minced garlic
- Freshly ground pepper, to taste
- Salt to taste

1. Pat the tilapia fillets dry with a paper towel.
2. Stir together the olive oil, chives, parsley, garlic, salt, and pepper in a small bowl.
3. Brush the mixture over the top of the tilapia fillets.
4. Place a crisper plate in each drawer. Add the fillets in a single layer to each drawer. Insert the drawers into the unit.
5. Select zone 1, then AIR FRY, then set the temperature to 360 degrees F/ 180 degrees C with a 20-minute timer. To match zone 2 settings to zone 1, choose MATCH. To begin, select START/STOP.
6. Remove the tilapia fillets from the drawers after the timer has finished.

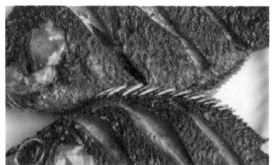

Scallops

Prep Time: 10 minutes | Cook Time: 5 minutes | Serves 4

- ½ cup Italian breadcrumbs
- ½ teaspoon garlic powder
- ¼ teaspoon salt
- ½ teaspoon black pepper
- 2 tablespoons butter, melted
- 1 pound sea scallops, rinsed and pat dry

1. Combine the breadcrumbs, garlic powder, salt, and pepper in a small bowl. Pour the melted butter into another shallow bowl.
2. Dredge each scallop in the melted butter, then roll it in the breadcrumb mixture until well covered.
3. Place a crisper plate in each drawer. Put the scallops in a single layer in each drawer. Insert the drawers into the unit.
   4. Select zone 1, then AIR FRY, then set the temperature to 360 degrees F/ 180 degrees C with a 5-minute timer. To match zone 2 settings to zone 1, choose MATCH. To begin, select START/STOP.
4. Press START/STOP to pause the unit when the timer reaches 3 minutes. Remove the drawers. Use tongs to carefully flip the scallops over. To resume cooking, re-insert the drawers into the unit and press START/STOP.
5. Remove the scallops from the drawers after the timer has finished.

Tuna Patties

Prep Time: 10 minutes | Cook Time: 10 minutes | Serves 6

FOR THE TUNA PATTIES

- 1 tablespoon extra-virgin olive oil
- 1 tablespoon butter
- ½ cup chopped onion
- ½ red bell pepper, chopped
- 1 teaspoon minced garlic
- 2 (7-ounce) cans or 3 (5-ounce) cans albacore tuna fish in water, drained
- 1 tablespoon lime juice
- 1 celery stalk, chopped
- ¼ cup chopped fresh parsley
- 3 tablespoons grated parmesan cheese
- ½ teaspoon dried oregano
- ¼ teaspoon salt
- Black pepper, to taste
- 1 teaspoon sriracha
- ½ cup panko crumbs
- 2 whisked eggs
- FOR THE CRUMB COATING
- ½ cup panko crumbs
- ¼ cup parmesan cheese
- Non-stick spray

1. In a skillet, heat the oil and butter over medium-high heat.
2. Sauté the onions, red bell pepper, and garlic for 5 to 7 minutes.
3. Drain the tuna from the cans thoroughly. Put the tuna in a large mixing bowl. Add the lime juice.
4. Add the sautéed vegetables to the mixing bowl.
5. Add the celery, parsley, and cheese. Combine well.
6. Add the oregano, salt, and pepper to taste. Mix well.
7. Add a dash of sriracha for a spicy kick and mix well.
8. Add the panko crumbs and mix well.
9. Mix in the eggs until the mixture is well combined. You can add an extra egg if necessary, but the tuna is usually wet enough that it isn't required. Form 6 patties from the mixture.
10. Refrigerate for 30 to 60 minutes (or even overnight).
11. Remove from refrigerator and coat with a mixture of the ½ cup of panko crumbs and ¼ cup of parmesan cheese.
12. Spray the tops of the coated patties with some non-stick cooking spray.
13. Place a crisper place in each drawer. Put 3 patties in each drawer. Insert the drawers into the unit.
14. Select zone 1, then AIR FRY, then set the temperature to 390 degrees F/ 200 degrees C with a 10-minute timer. To match zone 2 settings to zone 1, choose MATCH. To begin, select START/STOP.
15. Remove and garnish with chopped parsley.

Fish Tacos

Prep Time: 10 minutes | Cook Time: 30 minutes | Serves 5

- 1 pound firm white fish such as cod, haddock, pollock, halibut, or walleye
- ¾ cup gluten-free flour blend
- 3 eggs
- 1 cup gluten-free panko breadcrumbs
- 1 teaspoon garlic powder
- 1 teaspoon onion powder
- 1 teaspoon cumin
- 1 teaspoon lemon pepper
- 1 teaspoon red chili flakes
- 1 teaspoon kosher salt, divided
- 1 teaspoon pepper, divided
- Cooking oil spray
- 1 package corn tortillas
- Toppings such as tomatoes, avocado, cabbage, radishes, jalapenos, salsa, or hot sauce (optional)

1. Dry the fish with paper towels. (Make sure to thaw the fish if it's frozen.) Depending on the size of the fillets, cut the fish in half or thirds.
2. On both sides of the fish pieces, liberally season with salt and pepper.
3. Put the flour in a dish.
4. In a separate bowl, crack the eggs and whisk them together until well blended.
5. Put the panko breadcrumbs in another bowl. Add the garlic powder, onion powder, cumin, lemon pepper, and red chili flakes. Add salt and pepper to taste. Stir until everything is well blended.
6. Each piece of fish should be dipped in the flour, then the eggs, and finally in the breadcrumb mixture. Make sure that each piece is completely coated.
7. Put a crisper plate in each drawer. Arrange the fish pieces in a single layer in each drawer. Insert the drawers into the unit.
8. Select zone 1, then AIR FRY, then set the temperature to 360 degrees F/ 180 degrees C with a 20-minute timer. To match zone 2 settings to zone 1, choose MATCH. To begin, select START/STOP.
9. Remove the fish from the drawers after the timer has finished. Place the crispy fish on warmed tortillas.

Bang Bang Shrimp

Prep Time: 15 minutes | Cook Time: 20 minutes | Serves 4

FOR THE SHRIMP

- 1 cup corn starch
- Salt and pepper, to taste
- 2 pounds shrimp, peeled and deveined
- ½ to 1 cup buttermilk
- Cooking oil spray
- 1 large egg whisked with 1 teaspoon water
- FOR THE SAUCE
- 1/3 cup sweet Thai chili sauce
- ¼ cup sour cream
- ¼ cup mayonnaise
- 2 tablespoons buttermilk
- 1 tablespoon sriracha, or to taste
- Pinch dried dill weed

1. Season the corn starch with salt and pepper in a wide, shallow bowl.
2. In a large mixing bowl, toss the shrimp in the buttermilk to coat them.
3. Dredge the shrimp in the seasoned corn starch.
4. Brush with the egg wash after spraying with cooking oil.
5. Place a crisper plate in each drawer. Place the shrimp in a single layer in each. You may need to cook in batches.
6. Select zone 1, then AIR FRY, then set the temperature to 360 degrees F/ 180 degrees C with a 5-minute timer. To match zone 2 settings to zone 1, choose MATCH. To begin, select START/STOP.
7. Meanwhile, combine all the sauce ingredients together in a bowl.
8. Remove the shrimp when the cooking time is over.

Chapter 7
Vegetable Recipes

Baked Zucchini

Prep Time: 10 minutes| Cook Time: 20 minutes| Serves 4

- 1 tablespoon olive oil
- 1 zucchini, diced
- ½ cup breadcrumbs
- ¼ cup Parmesan cheese, grated
- 2 teaspoons dried thyme

1. Combine all the ingredients in a bowl.
2. Transfer to the air fryer basket.
3. Select bake function.
4. Bake at 250 degrees F for 20 to 30 minutes or until tender.

Lemon Butter Green Beans

Prep Time: 10 minutes |Cook Time: 15 minutes |Serves 6

- 1 lb. green beans, sliced
- 2 tablespoons olive oil
- 2 cloves garlic, minced
- 2 tablespoons lemon juice
- 1 tablespoon Parmesan cheese
- 2 tablespoons butter

1. Add green beans to the air fryer.
2. Select air fry setting.
3. Cook at 390 degrees F for 10 minutes, stirring once or twice.
4. In a pan over medium heat, add butter and cook garlic for 30 seconds.
5. Stir in the rest of the ingredients.
6. Cook for 1 minute.
7. Pour sauce over the green beans and serve.

Buffalo Cauliflower

Prep Time: 20 minutes| Cook Time: 15 minutes| Serves 6

- 1 head cauliflower, sliced into florets
- 1 tablespoon olive oil
- ¼ teaspoon cumin
- ¼ teaspoon garlic powder
- ½ teaspoon paprika
- ¼ teaspoon dry mustard
- ¼ teaspoon cayenne pepper
- 3 cloves garlic, minced
- 4 tablespoons butter
- 2 tablespoons lime juice
- 1 cup hot pepper sauce
- Pepper to taste

1. Toss cauliflower in olive oil.
2. Add to the air fryer basket.
3. Choose roast setting.
4. Cook at 400 degrees F for 7 minutes, stirring once or twice.
5. Mix buffalo sauce ingredients in a bowl.
6. Toss cauliflower in sauce.
7. Air fry for another 5 minutes.

Honey Roasted Carrots

Prep Time: 10 minutes | Cook Time: 20 minutes| Serves 4

- 3 cups baby carrots
- 1 tablespoon olive oil
- 1 tablespoon honey
- Salt and pepper to taste

1. Toss carrots in oil.
2. Drizzle with honey and sprinkle with salt and pepper.
3. Add to the air fryer basket.
4. Choose roast setting.
5. Cook at 390 degrees F for 20 minutes, stirring once.

Roasted Brussels Sprouts

Prep Time: 10 minutes| Cook Time: 15 minutes | Serves 4

- 1 lb. Brussels sprouts
- 1 tablespoon olive oil
- 1 teaspoon garlic salt
- Pepper to taste

1. Toss Brussels sprouts in olive oil.
2. Season with garlic salt and pepper.
3. Transfer to the air fryer basket.
4. Cook at 390 degrees F for 5 to 7 minutes per side.

Roasted Cabbage

Prep Time: 10 minutes |Cook Time: 8 minutes |Serves 4

- 1 head cabbage, sliced into quarters
- 1 tablespoon olive oil
- 1 teaspoon garlic powder
- 1 teaspoon red pepper flakes
- Salt and pepper to taste

1. Toss cabbage in olive oil.
2. Sprinkle with garlic powder, red pepper flakes, salt and pepper.
3. Add to the air fryer basket.
4. Select roast setting.
5. Cook at 350 degrees F for 4 minutes per side.

Onion Rings

Prep Time: 20 minutes | Cook Time: 10 minutes | Serves 6

- 1 cup flour
- Salt and pepper to taste
- 1 egg, beaten
- 1 cup buttermilk
- 1 tablespoon Parmesan cheese
- ½ cup breadcrumbs
- 2 onions, sliced into rings
- Cooking spray

1. Add flour, salt and pepper to a bowl.
2. In another bowl, mix egg and buttermilk.
3. Combine Parmesan cheese and breadcrumbs to another bowl.
4. Coat onion rings with flour, dip in egg and dredge with breadcrumb mixture.
5. Spray with oil.
6. Add to the air fryer basket.
7. Set it to air fry.
8. Cook at 400 degrees F for 5 minutes per side.

Veggie Burgers with "Fried" Onion Rings

Prep time: 20 minutes | Cook time: 25 minutes | Serves 4

FOR THE VEGGIE BURGERS

- 1 (15-ounce) can black beans, drained and rinsed
- ½ cup panko bread crumbs
- 1 large egg
- ¼ cup finely chopped red bell pepper
- ¼ cup frozen corn, thawed
- 1 tablespoon olive oil
- ½ teaspoon garlic powder
- ½ teaspoon ground cumin
- ¼ teaspoon smoked paprika
- Nonstick cooking spray
- 4 hamburger buns
- ¼ cup barbecue sauce, for serving
- FOR THE ONION RINGS
- 1 large sweet onion
- ½ cup all-purpose flour
- 2 large eggs
- 1 cup panko bread crumbs
- ½ teaspoon kosher salt
- Nonstick cooking spray

TO PREP THE VEGGIE BURGERS:

1. In a large bowl, mash the beans with a potato masher or a fork. Stir in the panko, egg, bell pepper, corn, oil, garlic powder, cumin, and smoked paprika. Mix well.
2. Shape the mixture into 4 patties. Spritz both sides of each patty with cooking spray.

TO PREP THE ONION RINGS:

1. Cut the onion into ½-inch-thick rings.
2. Set up a breading station with three small shallow bowls. Place the flour in the first bowl. In the second bowl, beat the eggs. Place the panko and salt in the third bowl.
3. Bread the onions rings in this order: First, dip them into the flour, coating both sides. Then, dip into the beaten egg. Finally, coat them in the panko. Spritz each with cooking spray.

TO COOK THE BURGERS AND ONION RINGS:

1. Install a crisper plate in each of the two baskets. Place 2 veggie burgers in the Zone 1 basket. Place the onion rings in the Zone 2 basket and insert both baskets in the unit.
2. Select Zone 1, select AIR FRY, set the temperature to 390°F, and set the timer to 25 minutes.
3. Select Zone 2, select AIR FRY, set the temperature to 375°F, and set the timer to 10 minutes. Select SMART FINISH.
4. Press START/PAUSE to begin cooking.
5. When the Zone 1 timer reads 10 minutes, press START/PAUSE. Remove the basket and use a silicone spatula to flip the burgers. Reinsert the basket and press START/PAUSE to resume cooking.
6. When the Zone 1 timer reads 10 minutes, press START/PAUSE. Remove the basket and transfer the burgers to a plate. Place the 2 remaining burgers in the basket. Reinsert the basket and press START/PAUSE to resume cooking.
7. When both timers read 5 minutes, press START/PAUSE. Remove the Zone 1 basket and flip the burgers, then reinsert the basket. Remove the Zone 2 basket and shake vigorously to rearrange the onion rings and separate any that have stuck together. Reinsert the basket and press START/PAUSE to resume cooking.
8. When cooking is complete, the veggie burgers should be cooked through and the onion rings golden brown.
9. Place 1 burger on each bun. Top with barbecue sauce and serve with onion rings on the side.

Parmesan Pickle Chips

Prep Time: 10 minutes | Cook Time: 10 minutes | Serves 4

- ¼ teaspoon dill weed
- ¼ cup Parmesan cheese
- ¼ cup breadcrumbs
- 2 eggs
- 1 jar dill pickles

1. Mix dill weed, Parmesan cheese and breadcrumbs in a bowl.
2. Beat eggs in another bowl.
3. Dip each dill pickle in the bowl with eggs.
4. Dredge with breadcrumb mixture.
5. Add to the air fryer basket.
6. Set it to air fry.
7. Cook at 390 degrees F for 4 to 5 minutes per side.

Vegetarian Mains

Prep time: 15 minutes|Cook time: 25 minutes|Serves 4

- FOR THE TOFU CUTLETS
- 1 (14-ounce) package extra-firm tofu, drained
- 1 cup panko bread crumbs
- ¼ cup grated pecorino romano or Parmesan cheese
- 1 teaspoon garlic powder
- 1 teaspoon onion powder
- ¼ teaspoon kosher salt
- 1 tablespoon vegetable oil
- 4 lemon wedges, for serving
- FOR THE BRUSSELS SPROUTS
- 1 pound Brussels sprouts, trimmed
- 1 tablespoon vegetable oil
- 2 tablespoons grated pecorino romano or Parmesan cheese
- ½ teaspoon freshly ground black pepper, plus more to taste
- ¼ teaspoon kosher salt

TO PREP THE TOFU:

1. Cut the tofu horizontally into 4 slabs.
2. In a shallow bowl, mix together the panko, cheese, garlic powder, onion powder, and salt. Press both sides of each tofu slab into the panko mixture. Drizzle both sides with the oil.

TO PREP THE BRUSSELS SPROUTS:

1. Cut the Brussels sprouts in half through the root end.
2. In a large bowl, combine the Brussels sprouts and olive oil. Mix to coat.

TO COOK THE TOFU CUTLETS AND BRUSSELS SPROUTS:

1. Install a crisper plate in each of the two baskets. Place the tofu cutlets in a single layer in the Zone 1 basket and insert the basket in the unit. Place the Brussels sprouts in the Zone 2 basket and insert the basket in the unit.
2. Select Zone 1, select AIR FRY, set the temperature to 400°F, and set the timer to 20 minutes.
3. Select Zone 2, select ROAST, set the temperature to 400°F, and set the timer to 25 minutes. Select SMART FINISH.
4. Press START/PAUSE to begin cooking.
5. When both timers read 5 minutes, press START/PAUSE. Remove the Zone 1 basket and use a pair of silicone-tipped tongs to flip the tofu cutlets, then reinsert the basket in the unit. Remove the Zone 2 basket and sprinkle the cheese and black pepper over the Brussels sprouts. Reinsert the basket and press START/PAUSE to resume cooking.
6. When cooking is complete, the tofu should be crisp and the Brussels sprouts tender and beginning to brown.
7. Squeeze the lemon wedges over the tofu cutlets. Stir the Brussels sprouts, then season with the salt and additional black pepper to taste.

Bacon & Cheese Corn

Prep Time: 10 minutes| Cook Time: 12 minutes| Serves 4

- 4 ears corn, sliced into 4
- ¼ cup butter, melted
- ½ ranch dressing mix
- 1 cup cheddar cheese, shredded
- 3 slices bacon, cooked crisp and crumbled

1. Brush corn with butter.
2. Sprinkle with ranch dressing mix and cheese.
3. Add to the air fryer basket.
4. Set it to air fry.
5. Cook at 390 degrees F for 10 minutes, flipping once or twice.
6. Sprinkle cheese on top.
7. Cook for another 2 minutes.
8. Sprinkle with bacon before serving.

Garlic Mushrooms

Prep Time: 10 minutes| Cook Time: 10 minutes |Serves 4

- 8 oz. mushrooms
- 1 tablespoon olive oil
- 1 tablespoon butter, melted
- 1 teaspoon garlic powder
- 1 teaspoon Worcestershire Sauce
- Salt and pepper to taste

1. Mix all the ingredients in a bowl.
2. Transfer to the air fryer basket.
3. Choose air fry setting.
4. Cook at 400 degrees F for 3 to 5 minutes per side.

Chapter 8
Holiday Specials

Lush Snack Mix

Prep time: 10 minutes | Cook time: 10 minutes | Serves 10

- 120 ml honey
- 3 tablespoons butter, melted
- 1 teaspoon salt
- 475 ml sesame sticks
- 475 ml pumpkin seeds
- 475 ml granola
- 235 ml cashews
- 475 ml crispy corn puff cereal
- 475 ml mini pretzel crisps

1. In a bowl, combine the honey, butter, and salt. In another bowl, mix the sesame sticks, pumpkin seeds, granola, cashews, corn puff cereal, and pretzel crisps.
2. Combine the contents of the two bowls.
3. Put the mixture in half into the two air fryer drawers and air fry at 190°C for 10 to 12 minutes to toast the snack mixture, shaking the drawers frequently.
4. Put the snack mix on a cookie sheet and allow it to cool fully. Serve immediately.

Eggnog Bread

Prep time: 10 minutes | Cook time: 18 minutes | Serves 6 to 8

- 235 ml flour, plus more for dusting
- 60 ml sugar
- 1 teaspoon baking powder
- ¼ teaspoon salt
- ¼ teaspoon nutmeg
- 120 ml eggnog
- 1 egg yolk
- 1 tablespoon plus 1 teaspoon butter, melted
- 60 ml pecans
- 60 ml chopped candied fruit (cherries, pineapple, or mixed fruits)
- Cooking spray

1. In a medium bowl, stir together the flour, sugar, baking powder, salt, and nutmeg.
2. Add eggnog, egg yolk, and butter. Mix well but do not beat.
3. Stir in nuts and fruit. Spray a baking pan with cooking spray and dust with flour.
4. Spread batter into prepared pan and place into the zone 1 drawer. Bake at 180°C for 18 minutes or until top is dark golden brown and bread starts to pull away from sides of pan. Serve immediately.

Mushroom and Green Bean Casserole

Prep time: 10 minutes | Cook time: 15 minutes | Serves 4

- 4 tablespoons unsalted butter
- 60 ml diced brown onion
- 120 ml chopped white mushrooms
- 120 ml double cream
- 30 g full fat soft white cheese
- 120 ml chicken broth
- ¼ teaspoon xanthan gum
- 450 g fresh green beans, edges trimmed
- 14 g pork crackling, finely ground

1. In a medium skillet over medium heat, melt the butter.
2. Sauté the onion and mushrooms until they become soft and fragrant, about 3 to 5 minutes. Add the double cream, soft white cheese, and broth to the pan.
3. Whisk until smooth. Bring to a boil and then reduce to a simmer. Sprinkle the xanthan gum into the pan and remove from heat. Chop the green beans into 2-inch pieces and place into a baking dish. Pour the sauce mixture over them and stir until coated.
4. Top the dish with minced pork crackling. Put the dish into the zone 1 air fryer drawer and bake at 160°C for 15 minutes.
5. Top will be golden and green beans fork-tender when fully cooked. Serve warm.

Air Fried Spicy Olives

Prep time: 10 minutes | Cook time: 5 minutes | Serves 4

- 340 g pitted black extra-large olives
- 60 ml plain flour
- 235 ml panko breadcrumbs
- 2 teaspoons dried thyme
- 1 teaspoon red pepper flakes
- 1 teaspoon smoked paprika
- 1 egg beaten with 1 tablespoon water
- Vegetable oil for spraying

1. Drain the olives and place them on a paper towel–lined plate to dry.
2. Put the flour on a plate. Combine the panko, thyme, red pepper flakes, and paprika on a separate plate.
3. Dip an olive in the flour, shaking off any excess, then coat with egg mixture. Dredge the olive in the panko mixture, pressing to make the crumbs adhere, and place the breaded olive on a platter.
4. Repeat with the remaining olives.
5. Spray the olives with oil and place them in a single layer in half into the two air fryer drawers. Air fry at 200°C for 5 minutes until the breading is browned and crispy. Serve warm.

Kale Salad Sushi Rolls with Sriracha Mayonnaise

Prep time: 10 minutes | Cook time: 10 minutes | Serves 12

- 350 ml chopped kale
- 1 tablespoon sesame seeds
- ¾ teaspoon soy sauce
- ¾ teaspoon toasted sesame oil
- ½ teaspoon rice vinegar
- ¼ teaspoon ginger
- ⅛ teaspoon garlic powder
- Sushi Rolls:
- 3 sheets sushi nori
- 1 batch cauliflower rice
- ½ avocado, sliced
- Sriracha Mayonnaise:
- 60 ml Sriracha sauce
- 60 ml vegan mayonnaise
- Coating:
- 120 ml panko breadcrumbs

1. In a medium bowl, toss all the ingredients for the salad together until well coated and set aside.
2. Place a sheet of nori on a clean work surface and spread the cauliflower rice in an even layer on the nori. Scoop 2 to 3 tablespoon of kale salad on the rice and spread over. Place 1 or 2 avocado slices on top.
3. Roll up the sushi, pressing gently to get a nice, tight roll. Repeat to make the remaining 2 rolls. In a bowl, stir together the Sriracha sauce and mayonnaise until smooth.
4. Add breadcrumbs to a separate bowl. Dredge the sushi rolls in Sriracha Mayonnaise, then roll in breadcrumbs till well coated.
5. Place the coated sushi rolls in the two air fryer drawers and air fry at 200°C for 10 minutes, or until golden brown and crispy.
6. Flip the sushi rolls gently halfway through to ensure even cooking. Transfer to a platter and rest for 5 minutes before slicing each roll into 8 pieces. Serve warm.

Hasselback Potatoes

Prep time: 5 minutes | Cook time: 50 minutes | Serves 4

- 4 russet or Maris Piper potatoes, peeled
- Salt and freshly ground black pepper, to taste
- 60 ml grated Parmesan cheese
- Cooking spray

1. Spray the zone 1 air fryer drawer lightly with cooking spray.
2. Make thin parallel cuts into each potato, ⅛-inch to ¼-inch apart, stopping at about ½ of the way through. The potato needs to stay intact along the bottom.
3. Spray the potatoes with cooking spray and use the hands or a silicone brush to completely coat the potatoes lightly in oil. Put the potatoes, sliced side up, in the zone 1 air fryer drawer in a single layer.

4. Leave a little room between each potato. Sprinkle the potatoes lightly with salt and black pepper. Air fry at 200°C for 20 minutes.
5. Reposition the potatoes and spritz lightly with cooking spray again. Air fry until the potatoes are fork-tender and crispy and browned, another 20 to 30 minutes. Sprinkle the potatoes with Parmesan cheese and serve.

Air Fried Blistered Tomatoes

Prep time: 5 minutes | Cook time: 10 minutes | Serves 4 to 6

- 900 g cherry tomatoes
- 2 tablespoons olive oil
- 2 teaspoons balsamic vinegar
- ½ teaspoon salt
- ½ teaspoon ground black pepper

1. Toss the cherry tomatoes with olive oil in a large bowl to coat well. Pour the tomatoes in a cake pan.
2. Put the cake pan into the zone 1 drawer. Air fry the cherry tomatoes at 200°C for 10 minutes or until the tomatoes are blistered and lightly wilted.
3. Shake the drawer halfway through. Transfer the blistered tomatoes to a large bowl and toss with balsamic vinegar, salt, and black pepper before serving.

Cinnamon Rolls with Cream Glaze

Prep time: 2 hours 15 minutes | Cook time: 10 minutes | Serves 8

- 450 g frozen bread dough, thawed
- 2 tablespoons melted butter
- 1½ tablespoons cinnamon
- 180 ml brown sugar
- Cooking spray
- Cream Glaze:
- 110 g soft white cheese
- ½ teaspoon vanilla extract
- 2 tablespoons melted butter
- 300 ml powdered erythritol

1. Place the bread dough on a clean work surface, then roll the dough out into a rectangle with a rolling pin. Brush the top of the dough with melted butter and leave 1-inch edges uncovered.
2. Combine the cinnamon and sugar in a small bowl, then sprinkle the dough with the cinnamon mixture.
3. Roll the dough over tightly, then cut the dough log into 8 portions. Wrap the portions in plastic, better separately, and let sit to rise for 1 or 2 hours.
4. Meanwhile, combine the ingredients for the glaze in a separate small bowl. Stir to mix well. Spritz the two air fryer drawers with cooking spray.
5. Transfer the risen rolls in half into the two air fryer drawer. Air fry at 180°C for 5 minutes or until golden brown. Flip the rolls halfway through. Serve the rolls with the glaze.

Simple Butter Cake

Prep time: 25 minutes | Cook time: 20 minutes | Serves 8

- 235 ml plain flour
- 1¼ teaspoons baking powder
- ¼ teaspoon salt
- 120 ml plus 1½ tablespoons granulated white sugar
- 9½ tablespoons butter, at room temperature
- 2 large eggs
- 1 large egg yolk
- 2½ tablespoons milk
- 1 teaspoon vanilla extract
- Cooking spray

1. Spritz a cake pan with cooking spray. Combine the flour, baking powder, and salt in a large bowl. Stir to mix well. Whip the sugar and butter in a separate bowl with a hand mixer on medium speed for 3 minutes.
2. Whip the eggs, egg yolk, milk, and vanilla extract into the sugar and butter mix with a hand mixer. Pour in the flour mixture and whip with hand mixer until sanity and smooth.
3. Scrape the batter into the cake pan and level the batter with a spatula. Place the cake pan into the zone 1 drawer. Select Bake button and adjust temperature to 165°C, set time to 20 minutes and press Start.
4. Check the doneness during the last 5 minutes of the baking. Until a toothpick inserted in the centre comes out clean, invert the cake on a cooling rack and allow to cool for 15 minutes before slicing to serve.

Classic Churros

Prep time: 35 minutes | Cook time: 10 minutes per batch | Makes 12 churros

- 4 tablespoons butter
- ¼ teaspoon salt
- 120 ml water
- 120 ml plain flour
- 2 large eggs
- 2 teaspoons ground cinnamon
- 60 ml granulated white sugar
- Cooking spray

1. Put the butter, salt, and water in a saucepan. Bring to a boil until the butter is melted on high heat. Keep stirring.
2. Reduce the heat to medium and fold in the flour to form a dough. Keep cooking and stirring until the dough is dried out and coat the pan with a crust.
3. Turn off the heat and scrape the dough in a large bowl. Allow to cool for 15 minutes. Break and whisk the eggs into the dough with a hand mixer until the dough is sanity and firm enough to shape.
4. Scoop up 1 tablespoon of the dough and roll it into a ½-inch-diameter and 2-inch-long cylinder.
5. Repeat with remaining dough to make 12

cylinders in total. Combine the cinnamon and sugar in a large bowl and dunk the cylinders into the cinnamon mix to coat.
6. Arrange the cylinders on a plate and refrigerate for 20 minutes. Spritz the two air fryer drawers with cooking spray.
7. Place the cylinders in half into the two air fryer drawers and spritz with cooking spray. Air fry at 190°C for 10 minutes or until golden brown and fluffy. Flip them halfway through. Serve immediately.

Fried Dill Pickles with Buttermilk Dressing

Prep time: 45 minutes | Cook time: 8 minutes | Serves 6 to 8

- 60 ml buttermilk
- 60 ml chopped spring onions
- 180 ml mayonnaise
- 120 ml sour cream
- ½ teaspoon cayenne pepper
- ½ teaspoon onion powder
- ½ teaspoon garlic powder
- 1 tablespoon chopped chives
- 2 tablespoons chopped fresh dill
- Rock salt and ground black pepper, to taste
- Fried Dill Pickles:
- 180 ml plain flour
- 1 (900 g) jar kosher dill pickles, cut into 4 spears, drained
- 600 ml panko breadcrumbs
- 2 eggs, beaten with 2 tablespoons water
- Rock salt and ground black pepper, to taste
- Cooking spray

1. Combine the ingredients for the dressing in a bowl. Stir to mix well. Wrap the bowl in plastic and refrigerate for 30 minutes or until ready to serve.
2. Pour the flour in a bowl and sprinkle with salt and ground black pepper. Stir to mix well. Put the breadcrumbs in a separate bowl.
3. Pour the beaten eggs in a third bowl. Dredge the pickle spears in the flour, then into the eggs, and then into the panko to coat well.
4. Shake the excess off. Arrange the pickle spears in a single layer in the two air fryer drawers and spritz with cooking spray. Air fry at 200°C for 8 minutes. Flip the pickle spears halfway through. Serve the pickle spears with buttermilk dressing.

Prawns with Sriracha and Worcestershire Sauce

Prep time: 15 minutes | Cook time: 10 minutes per batch | Serves 4

- 1 tablespoon Sriracha sauce
- 1 teaspoon Worcestershire sauce
- 2 tablespoons sweet chilli sauce
- 180 ml mayonnaise
- 1 egg, beaten
- 235 ml panko breadcrumbs
- 450 g raw prawns, shelled and deveined, rinsed and drained
- Lime wedges, for serving
- Cooking spray

1. Spritz the two air fryer drawers with cooking spray.
2. Combine the Sriracha sauce,Worcestershire sauce, chilli sauce, and mayo in a bowl. Stir to mix well.
3. Reserve 80 ml the mixture as the dipping sauce. Combine the remaining sauce mixture with the beaten egg. Stir to mix well.
4. Put the panko in a separate bowl. Dredge the prawns in the sauce mixture first, then into the panko. Roll the prawns to coat well.
5. Shake the excess off. Place the prawns in half into the two air fryer drawers, then spritz with cooking spray. Air fry the prawns at 180°C for 10 minutes or until opaque.
6. Flip the prawns halfway through the cooking time. Remove the prawns from the air fryer and serve with reserve sauce mixture and squeeze the lime wedges over.

Golden Nuggets

Prep time: 15 minutes | Cook time: 4 minutes per batch | Makes 20 nuggets

- 235 ml plain flour, plus more for dusting
- 1 teaspoon baking powder
- ½ teaspoon butter, at room temperature, plus more for brushing
- ¼ teaspoon salt
- 60 ml water
- ⅛ teaspoon onion powder
- ¼ teaspoon garlic powder
- ⅛ teaspoon seasoning salt
- Cooking spray

1. Line the two air fryer drawers with parchment paper. Mix the flour, baking powder, butter, and salt in a large bowl. Stir to mix well.
2. Gradually whisk in the water until a sanity dough forms. Put the dough on a lightly floured work surface, then roll it out into a ½-inch thick rectangle with a rolling pin.
3. Cut the dough into about twenty 1- or 2-inch squares, then arrange the squares in a single layer in the two air fryer drawers. Spritz with cooking spray.
4. Combine onion powder, garlic powder, and

seasoning salt in a small bowl. Stir to mix well, then sprinkle the squares with the powder mixture.
5. Air fry the dough squares at 190°C for 4 minutes or until golden brown. Flip the squares halfway through the cooking time.
6. Remove the golden nuggets from the air fryer and brush with more butter immediately. Serve warm.

Jewish Blintzes

Prep time: 5 minutes | Cook time: 10 minutes | Makes 8 blintzes

- 2 (213 g) packages farmer or ricotta cheese, mashed
- 60 ml soft white cheese
- ¼ teaspoon vanilla extract
- 60 ml granulated white sugar
- 8 egg roll wrappers
- 4 tablespoons butter, melted

1. Combine the cheese, soft white cheese, vanilla extract, and sugar in a bowl.
2. Stir to mix well. Unfold the egg roll wrappers on a clean work surface, spread 60 ml filling at the edge of each wrapper and leave a ½-inch edge uncovering.
3. Wet the edges of the wrappers with water and fold the uncovered edge over the filling. Fold the left and right sides in the centre, then tuck the edge under the filling and fold to wrap the filling.
4. Brush the wrappers with melted butter, then arrange the wrappers in a single layer in the two air fryer drawers, seam side down. Leave a little space between each two wrappers. Air fry at 190°C for 10 minutes or until golden brown. Serve immediately.

Mexican Pizza

Prep time: 10 minutes | Cook time: 7 to 9 minutes | Serves 4

- 180 ml refried beans
- 120 ml salsa
- 10 frozen precooked beef meatballs, thawed and sliced
- 1 jalapeño pepper, sliced
- 4 wholemeal pitta breads
- 235 ml shredded pepper Jack or Monterey Jack cheese
- 120 ml shredded Colby or Gouda cheese
- 80 ml sour cream

1. In a medium bowl, combine the refried beans, salsa, meatballs, and jalapeño pepper.
2. Top the pittas with the refried bean mixture and sprinkle with the cheeses.
3. Place into the zone 1 drawer. Select Bake button and adjust temperature to 190°C, set time to 8 to 10 minutes and press Start. Until the pizza is crisp and the cheese is melted and starts to brown, top each pizza with a dollop of sour cream and serve warm.

Chapter 9
Snacks and Appetizers Recipes

Chicken Crescent Wraps

Prep Time: 10 minutes | Cook Time: 12 minutes | Serve 6

- 3 tablespoons chopped onion
- 3 garlic cloves, peeled and minced
- ¾ (8 ounces) package cream cheese
- 6 tablespoons butter
- 2 boneless chicken breasts, cubed, cooked
- 3 (10 ounces) cans refrigerated crescent roll dough

1. Heat oil in a skillet and add onion and garlic to sauté until soft.
2. Add cooked chicken, sautéed veggies, butter, and cream cheese to a blender.
3. Blend well until smooth. Spread the crescent dough over a flat surface.
4. Slice the dough into 12 rectangles.
5. Spoon the chicken mixture at the center of each rectangle.
6. Roll the dough to wrap the mixture and form a ball.
7. Divide these balls into the two crisper plate.
8. Return the crisper plate to the Ninja Foodi Dual Zone Air Fryer.
9. Choose the Air Fry mode for Zone 1 and set the temperature to 390 degrees F/ 200 degrees C and the time to 12 minutes.
10. Select the "MATCH" button to copy the settings for Zone 2.
11. Initiate cooking by pressing the START/STOP button.
12. Serve warm.

Potato Tater Tots

Prep Time: 10 minutes | Cook Time: 27 minutes | Serves 4

- 2 potatoes, peeled
- ½ teaspoon Cajun seasoning
- Olive oil cooking spray
- Sea salt to taste

1. Boil water in a cooking pot and cook potatoes in it for 15 minutes.
2. Drain and leave the potatoes to cool in a bowl.
3. Grate these potatoes and toss them with Cajun seasoning.
4. Make small tater tots out of this mixture.
5. Divide them into the two crisper plates and spray them with cooking oil.
6. Return the crisper plates to the Ninja Foodi Dual Zone Air Fryer.
7. Choose the Air Fry mode for Zone 1 and set the temperature to 375 degrees F/ 190 degrees C and the time to 27 minutes.
8. Select the "MATCH" button to copy the settings for Zone 2.
9. Initiate cooking by pressing the START/STOP button.
10. Flip them once cooked halfway through, and resume cooking.
11. Serve warm

Blueberries Muffins

Prep Time: 15 Minutes | Cook Time: 15 Minutes | Serves 2

- Salt, 1 pinch
- 2 eggs
- ⅓ cup sugar
- ⅓ cup vegetable oil
- 4 tablespoons water
- 1 teaspoon lemon zest
- ¼ teaspoon vanilla extract
- ½ teaspoon baking powder
- 1 cup all-purpose flour
- 1 cup blueberries

1. Take 4 ramekins that are oven safe and layer them with muffin papers.
2. Take a bowl and whisk the egg, sugar, oil, water, vanilla extract, and lemon zest in.
3. Whisk it all very well.
4. In a separate bowl, mix the flour, baking powder, and salt.
5. Add the dry ingredients slowly to the wet ingredients.
6. Pour the batter into the ramekins and top with blueberries.
7. Divide them between both zones of the Ninja Foodi 2-Basket Air Fryer.
8. Set the time for zone 1 to 15 minutes at 350 degrees F/ 175 degrees C on AIR FRY mode.
9. Select the MATCH button for the zone 2 basket.
10. Check if not done, and let it AIR FRY for one more minute.
11. Once it is done, serve.

Crispy Plantain Chips

Prep Time: 15 minutes | Cook Time: 20 minutes | Serves 4

- 1 green plantain
- 1 teaspoon canola oil
- ½ teaspoon sea salt

1. Peel and cut the plantains into long strips using a mandolin slicer.
2. Grease the crisper plates with ½ teaspoon of canola oil.
3. Toss the plantains with salt and remaining canola oil.
4. Divide these plantains in the two crisper plates.
5. Return the crisper plate to the Ninja Foodi Dual Zone Air Fryer.
6. Choose the Air Fry mode for Zone 1 and set the temperature to 350 degrees F/ 175 degrees C and the time to 20 minutes.
7. Select the "MATCH" button to copy the settings for Zone 2.
8. Initiate cooking by pressing the START/STOP button.
9. Toss the plantains after 10 minutes and resume cooking.
10. Serve warm.

Peppered Asparagus

Prep Time: 10 minutes| Cook Time: 16 minutes | Serves 6

- 1 bunch of asparagus, trimmed
- Avocado or Olive Oil
- Himalayan salt, to taste
- Black pepper, to taste

1. Divide the asparagus in the two crisper plate.
2. Toss the asparagus with salt, black pepper, and oil.
3. Return the crisper plate to the Ninja Foodi Dual Zone Air Fryer.
4. Choose the Air Fry mode for Zone 1 and set the temperature to 390 degrees F/ 200 degrees C and the time to 16 minutes.
5. Select the "MATCH" button to copy the settings for Zone 2.
6. Initiate cooking by pressing the START/STOP button.
7. Serve warm.

Cauliflower Gnocchi

Prep Time: 15 minutes| Cook Time: 17 minutes| Serves 5

- 1 bag frozen cauliflower gnocchi
- 1 ½ tablespoons olive oil
- 1 teaspoon garlic powder
- 3 tablespoons parmesan, grated
- ½ teaspoon dried basil
- Salt to taste
- Fresh chopped parsley for topping

1. Toss gnocchi with olive oil, garlic powder, 1 tablespoon of parmesan, salt, and basil in a bowl.
2. Divide the gnocchi in the two crisper plate.
3. Return the crisper plate to the Ninja Foodi Dual Zone Air Fryer.
4. Choose the Air Fry mode for Zone 1 and set the temperature to 400 degrees F/ 200 degrees C and the time to 10 minutes.
5. Select the "MATCH" button to copy the settings for Zone 2.
6. Initiate cooking by pressing the START/STOP button.
7. Toss the gnocchi once cooked halfway through, then resume cooking.
8. Drizzle the remaining parmesan on top of the gnocchi and cook again for 7 minutes.
9. Serve warm.

Chicken Tenders

Prep Time: 15 Minutes | Cook Time: 12 Minutes | Serves 3

- 1 pound chicken tenders
- Salt and black pepper, to taste
- 1 cup Panko bread crumbs
- 2 cups Italian bread crumbs
- 1 cup Parmesan cheese
- 2 eggs
- Oil spray, for greasing

1. Sprinkle the tenders with salt and black pepper.
2. In a medium bowl mix the Panko bread crumbs with Italian bread crumbs.
3. Add salt, pepper, and Parmesan cheese.
4. Crack two eggs into a bowl.
5. Dip the chicken tenders into the eggs and then into the bread crumbs and spray with oil spray.
6. Line both of the baskets of the air fryer with parchment paper.
7. Divide the tenders between the baskets of Ninja Foodi 2-Basket Air Fryer.
8. Set zone 1 basket to AIR FRY mode at 350 degrees F/ 175 degrees C for 12 minutes.
9. Select the MATCH button for the zone 2 basket.
10. Once it's done, serve.

Grill Cheese Sandwich

Prep Time: 15 Minutes | Cook Time: 10 Minutes | Serves 2

- 4 white bread slices
- 2 tablespoons butter, melted
- 2 slices sharp Cheddar
- 2 slices Swiss cheese
- 2 slices Mozzarella cheese

1. Brush melted butter on one side of all the bread slices and then top the 2 bread slices with Cheddar, Swiss, and mozzarella.
2. Top it with the other slice to make a sandwich.
3. Divide it between the two baskets of the air fryer.
4. Turn toAIR FRY mode for zone 1 basket at 350 degrees F/ 175 degrees C for 10 minutes.
5. Use the MATCH button for zone 2.
6. Once done, serve.

Parmesan French Fries

Prep Time: 10 minutes| Cook Time: 20 minutes | Serves 6

- 3 medium russet potatoes
- 2 tablespoons parmesan cheese
- 2 tablespoons fresh parsley, chopped
- 1 tablespoon olive oil
- Salt, to taste

1. Wash the potatoes and pass them through the fries' cutter to get ¼-inch-thick fries.
2. Place the fries in a colander and drizzle salt on top.
3. Leave these fries for 10 minutes, then rinse.
4. Toss the potatoes with parmesan cheese, oil, salt, and parsley in a bowl.
5. Divide the potatoes into the two crisper plates.
6. Return the crisper plates to the Ninja Foodi Dual Zone Air Fryer.
7. Choose the Air Fry mode for Zone 1 and set the temperature to 360 degrees F/ 180 degrees C and the time to 20 minutes.
8. Select the "MATCH" button to copy the settings for Zone 2.
9. Initiate cooking by pressing the START/STOP button.
10. Toss the chips once cooked halfway through, then resume cooking.
11. Serve warm.

Spicy Chicken Tenders

Prep Time: 15 Minutes | Cook Time: 12 Minutes | Serves 2

- 2 large eggs, whisked
- 2 tablespoons lemon juice
- Salt and black pepper
- 1 pound chicken tenders
- 1 cup Panko bread crumbs
- ½ cup Italian bread crumbs
- 1 teaspoon smoked Paprika
- ¼ teaspoon garlic powder
- ¼ teaspoon onion powder
- ½ cup fresh grated Parmesan cheese

1. Take a bowl and whisk the eggs and set aside.
2. In a large bowl, add lemon juice, Paprika, salt, black pepper, garlic powder, onion powder
3. In a separate bowl, mix Panko bread crumbs, Italian bread crumbs, and Parmesan cheese.
4. Dip the chicken tenders in the spice mixture and coat well.
5. Let the tenders sit for 1 hour.
6. Dip each tender into the egg mixture and then into the bread crumbs.
7. Line both the baskets of the air fryer with parchment paper.
8. Divide the tenders between the baskets.
9. Set zone 1 basket to AIR FRY mode at 350 degrees F/ 175 degrees C for 12 minutes.
10. Select the MATCH button for the zone 2 basket.
11. Once it's done, serve.

Crispy Tortilla Chips

Prep Time: 15 minutes | Cook Time: 13 minutes | Serves 8

- 4 (6-inch) corn tortillas
- 1 tablespoon Avocado Oil
- Sea salt to taste
- Cooking spray

1. Spread the corn tortillas on the working surface.
2. Slice them into bite-sized triangles.
3. Toss them with salt and cooking oil.
4. Divide the triangles in the two crisper plates into a single layer.
5. Return the crisper plates to the Ninja Foodi Dual Zone Air Fryer.
6. Choose the Air Fry mode for Zone 1 and set the temperature to 390 degrees F/ 200 degrees C and the time to 13 minutes.
7. Select the "MATCH" button to copy the settings for Zone 2.
8. Initiate cooking by pressing the START/STOP button.
9. Toss the chips once cooked halfway through, then resume cooking.
10. Serve and enjoy.

Strawberries and Walnuts Muffins

Prep Time: 15 Minutes | Cook Time: 15 Minutes | Serves 2

- Salt, pinch
- 2 eggs, whisked
- ⅓ cup maple syrup
- ⅓ cup coconut oil
- 4 tablespoons water
- 1 teaspoon orange zest
- ¼ teaspoon vanilla extract
- ½ teaspoon baking powder
- 1 cup all-purpose flour
- 1 cup strawberries, finely chopped
- ⅓ cup walnuts, chopped and roasted

1. Layer 4 ramekins with muffin paper.
2. Add egg, maple syrup, oil, water, vanilla extract, and orange zest to a bowl and mix well.
3. In a separate bowl, mix flour, baking powder, and salt.
4. Add the dry ingredients slowly to the wet ingredients.
5. Pour the batter into the ramekins and top with strawberries and walnuts.
6. Divide the ramekins into both zones. For zone 1, set to AIR FRY mode at 350 degrees F/ 175 degrees C for 15 minutes.
7. Select the MATCH button for the zone 2 basket.
8. Check and if not done, let it AIR FRY for one more minute.
9. Once done, serve.

Cheddar Quiche

Prep Time: 10 Minutes | Cook Time: 12 Minutes | Serves 2

- 4 eggs, organic
- 1-¼ cup heavy cream
- Salt, pinch
- ½ cup broccoli florets
- ½ cup Cheddar cheese, shredded and for sprinkling

1. Take a Pyrex pitcher and crack two eggs into it.
2. Fill it with heavy cream, about half the way up.
3. Add in the salt and then the broccoli.
4. Pour the mixture into two quiche dishes, and top it with shredded Cheddar cheese.
5. Divide it into both zones of the baskets.
6. For zone 1, set the time to 10-12 minutes at 325 degrees F/ 160 degrees C on AIR FRY mode.
7. Select the MATCH button for the zone 2 basket.
8. Once done, serve hot.

Dijon Cheese Sandwich

Prep Time: 10 Minutes | Cook Time: 10 Minutes | Serves 2

- 4 large slices sourdough, whole grain
- 4 tablespoons Dijon mustard
- 1-½ cup grated sharp Cheddar cheese
- 2 teaspoons green onion, green part chopped off
- 2 tablespoons butter melted

1. Brush the melted butter on one side of all the bread slices.
2. Spread Dijon mustard on the other side of the slices.
3. Top the 2 bread slices with Cheddar cheese and top it with green onions.
4. Cover with the remaining two slices to make two sandwiches.
5. Place one sandwich in each basket of the air fryer.
6. Turn to AIR FRY mode for zone 1 basket at 350 degrees F/ 175 degrees C for 10 minutes.
7. Use the MATCH button for zone 2.
8. Once it's done, serve.

Appendix 1 Measurement Conversion Chart

WEIGHT EQUIVALENTS	
US STANDARD	**METRIC (APPROXIMATE)**
1 ounce	28 g
2 ounces	57 g
5 ounces	142 g
10 ounces	284 g
15 ounces	425 g
16 ounces (1 pound)	455 g
1.5pounds	680 g
2pounds	907 g

VOLUME EQUIVALENTS (DRY)	
US STANDARD	**METRIC (APPROXIMATE)**
⅛ teaspoon	0.5 mL
¼ teaspoon	1 mL
½ teaspoon	2 mL
¾ teaspoon	4 mL
1 teaspoon	5 mL
1 tablespoon	15 mL
¼ cup	59 mL
½ cup	118 mL
¾ cup	177 mL
1 cup	235 mL
2 cups	475 mL
3 cups	700 mL
4 cups	1 L

TEMPERATURES EQUIVALENTS	
FAHRENHEIT (F)	**CELSIUS (C) (APPROXIMATE)**
225 °F	107 °C
250 °F	120 °C
275 °F	135 °C
300 °F	150 °C
325 °F	160 °C
350 °F	180 °C
375 °F	190 °C
400 °F	205 °C
425 °F	220 °C
450 °F	235 °C
475 °F	245 °C
500 °F	260 °C

VOLUME EQUIVALENTS (LIQUID)		
US STANDARD	**US STANDARD (OUNCES)**	**US STANDARD (OUNCES)**
2 tablespoons	1 fl.oz	30 mL
¼ cup	2 fl.oz	60 mL
½ cup	4 fl.oz	120 mL
1 cup	8 fl.oz	240 mL
1½ cup	12 fl.oz	355 mL
2 cups or 1 pint	16 fl.oz	475 mL
4 cups or 1 quart	32 fl.oz	1 L

Appendix 2 Air Fryer Cooking Chart

Meat and Seafood	Temp	Time (min)
Bacon	400°F	5 to 10
Beef Eye Round Roast (4 lbs.)	390°F	45 to 55
Bone to in Pork Chops	400°F	4 to 5 per side
Brats	400°F	8 to 10
Burgers	350°F	8 to 10
Chicken Breast	375°F	22 to 23
Chicken Tender	400°F	14 to 16
Chicken Thigh	400°F	25
Chicken Wings (2 lbs.)	400°F	10 to 12
Cod	370°F	8 to 10
Fillet Mignon (8 oz.)	400°F	14 to 18
Fish Fillet (0.5 lb., 1-inch)	400°F	10
Flank Steak (1.5 lbs.)	400°F	10 to 14
Lobster Tails (4 oz.)	380°F	5 to 7
Meatballs	400°F	7 to 10
Meat Loaf	325°F	35 to 45
Pork Chops	375°F	12 to 15
Salmon	400°F	5 to 7
Salmon Fillet (6 oz.)	380°F	12
Sausage Patties	400°F	8 to 10
Shrimp	375°F	8
Steak	400°F	7 to 14
Tilapia	400°F	8 to 12
Turkey Breast (3 lbs.)	360°F	40 to 50
Whole Chicken (6.5 lbs.)	360°F	75

Frozen Foods	Temp	Time (min)
Breaded Shrimp	400°F	9
Chicken Burger	360°F	11
Chicken Nudgets	400°F	10
Corn Dogs	400°F	7
Curly Fries (1 to 2 lbs.)	400°F	11 to 14
Fish Sticks (10 oz.)	400°F	10
French Fries	380°F	15 to 20
Hash Brown	360°F	15 to 18
Meatballs	380°F	6 to 8
Mozzarella Sticks	400°F	8
Onion Rings (8 oz.)	400°F	8
Pizza	390°F	5 to 10
Pot Pie	360°F	25
Pot Sticks (10 oz.)	400°F	8
Sausage Rolls	400°F	15
Spring Rolls	400°F	15 to 20

Vegetables	Temp	Time (min)
Asparagus	375°F	4 to 6
Baked Potatoes	400°F	35 to 45
Broccoli	400°F	8 to 10
Brussels Sprouts	350°F	15 to 18
Butternut Squash (cubed)	375°F	20 to 25
Carrots	375°F	15 to 25
Cauliflower	400°F	10 to 12
Corn on the Cob	390°F	6
Eggplant	400°F	15
Green Beans	375°F	16 to 20
Kale	250°F	12
Mushrooms	400°F	5
Peppers	375°F	8 to 10
Sweet Potatoes (whole)	380°F	30 to 35
Tomatoes (halved, sliced)	350°F	10
Zucchini (½-inch sticks)	400°F	12

Desserts	Temp	Time (min)
Apple Pie	320°F	30
Brownies	350°F	17
Churros	360°F	13
Cookies	350°F	5
Cupcakes	330°F	11
Doughnuts	360°F	5
Roasted Bananas	375°F	8
Peaches	350°F	5

Appendix 3 Index

SANDRA D. FENLEY

Made in the USA
Las Vegas, NV
06 January 2024

84011046R00044